POSTAL REORGANIZATION

POSTAL REORGANIZATION

Managing the Public's Business

JOHN T. TIERNEY
Georgetown University

Auburn House Publishing Company
Boston, Massachusetts

Library of Congress Cataloging in Publication Data
Tierney, John T. 1951–
    Postal reorganization.
    Includes index.
    1. United States Postal Service—Management.
    2. Government business enterprises—United States—Management—Case
    studies. 3. Administrative agencies—United States—Management—Case
    studies. I. Title.
HE6371.T5   353.0087'3   80-26905
ISBN 0-86569-061-8

Printed in the United States of America

*To my parents, Betty and Tom Tierney,
for their support, their encouragement,
and their example.*

PREFACE

This is a study of the management of the nation's oldest and largest public business—the U.S. postal system. The book aims primarily to analyze and explain what difference the 1971 reorganization of the U.S. Post Office Department has made in how the huge mail delivery organization is managed.

My purpose in offering this analysis is neither to catalogue the perceived weaknesses of postal management nor to offer prescriptions for improving the system's performance. Rather, I am trying to identify and explain what features of the Postal Service's task and environment make it difficult for the organization's executives to apply "businesslike" solutions to the postal system's problems. It is my hope that this study will clear away some of the fog of popular misunderstanding that surrounds public bureaucracies in general and the Postal Service in particular. As the following pages document, much of what citizens regard as inefficiency or ineffectiveness in the operation of public agencies stems not from managerial incompetence but from the obligation of most government agencies to pursue multiple goals and to serve multiple interests, all of which may be conflicting or even irreconcilable.

Readers predisposed to believe that the mail system faces problems because postal managers are incompetent, prodigal, or stupid may find this book's explanations of those problems too sympathetic. So be it. If anything, I have come away from this study impressed by the intelligence, the expertise, and the diligence of postal managers and executives. These are skilled people performing a more complex job than most outsiders would expect, and operating in a political environment that—despite the sweeping reorganization of 1971—still poses serious constraints on their ability to satisfy simultaneously all elements of the public or to apply efficient and effective means of improving performance.

I undertook this study with many interests in mind. First, the sweeping 1971 postal reorganization presented an unusual research opportunity, the chance to determine what effect substantial changes in the political and administrative structures governing an agency would have on its behavior. Here was a significant alteration in the managerial environment of an important governmental enterprise—a reorganization carried out with immodest expectations for its eventual success. When I began this research several years ago, the dominant view seemed to be that the reorganization had failed miserably to meet the expectations of its architects. I was interested in determining whether this interpretation was true and if so, what might account for the alleged failures. I have discovered successes as well as failures, some predictable, some not.

Second, I was interested in studying the Postal Service and the political environment in which it is managed because the literature on government enterprises is so sparse. The Postal Service, for example, has been studied by a few economists but has received almost no attention from political scientists or students of public administration. That struck me as curious, because of the size and political clout of the Postal Service's 630,000-member workforce, and the political importance of organizations affected by unpopular postal rate increases (especially magazine publishers and direct-mail advertisers), and also because the Postal Service is one of the few federal agencies to touch directly the lives of most Americans on an almost daily basis.

Moreover, I wanted to describe and analyze the management and political environment of the reconstituted Postal Service, because in my view, far too much of the literature that does exist on the postal system focuses on whether the federal government should continue to have a monopoly on delivering letter mail. For years there have been calls from one corner or another (most recently from free-market economists) for an end to the government's historic monopoly on letter mail. It is decidedly not my task here to explore further the costs and benefits of such a move. I leave that to others. I have undertaken this study instead in the belief that we know far too little about how the postal system is run *now*, much less how it might operate under even more radically altered arrangements. My task has been to examine the management of the Postal Service in its governmental setting. Readers who expect that such an analysis must conclude favoring greater competition or diversion to private industry may be disappointed. Rather, in light of what we shall learn about the Postal Service, we shall be able to assess more realistically the likelihood that additional changes— such as repeal of the monopoly on letter mail—will produce significant benefits in money savings or more efficient services. We shall find reasons to doubt that there is some magic formula for producing what the public apparently wants: fast, frequent mail delivery in all parts of the country at uniformly low prices.

I have approached this study as a political scientist, not as an investigative reporter, an economist, or a management analyst. The method of inquiry was eclectic, involving many of the standard research techniques of political scientists. It included reading histories, scrutinizing statutes, examining administrative structures, compiling and interpreting statements of postal policy, examining internal memoranda, perusing manuals and hearings and reports, surveying mailers' association and postal union newsletters, gathering evaluations and criticisms of organizational performance, visiting postal facilities, and conducting personal interviews with persons inside the Postal Service, on Capitol Hill, and with the postal unions and special mailers' organizations. To those persons who granted me interviews or who assisted me in gathering data, I extend my thanks.

In conducting the research and in writing the book, I have benefited greatly from the continuing advice and support of Professor James Q. Wilson of Harvard University. Not only has he done much to shape my thinking about governmental agencies (an acknowledgment I want to make without in any way implicating him in the following analysis of the Postal Service), but he was helpful to me at every stage of this project, repeatedly coming through with various kinds of support—intellectual, financial, and moral— just when they were most needed. I have him to thank as well for the generous financial support I received from the Alfred P. Sloan Foundation and its program at Harvard to encourage the study of public management.

Professor Francis E. Rourke of The Johns Hopkins University first got me interested in studying federal agencies. He has generously paid for that transgression many times over by his friendship and most recently by giving parts of this manuscript a helpful reading.

My thanks to John Harney, Gene Bailey, and David Johnson of Auburn House for their unflagging goodwill, help, and encouragement.

I owe special thanks to Patricia Rachal, my friend and colleague, whose contribution to this work I can gratefully, but not adequately, acknowledge. She has been a caring listener and a knowing critic from the conception of this project to its completion.

J.T.T.
WASHINGTON, D.C.

CONTENTS

INTRODUCTION

The United States Postal Service, created in 1971 out of the ribs of the old Post Office Department, is a monument to the capacity of the American government to change. The Postal Reorganization Act of 1970 produced the most thorough reconstruction of postal administration in nearly two centuries. It removed the postal department from the President's cabinet, ended the authority of Congress and the White House to set employee wages and postage rates, bestowed on the new Postal Service its own personnel system, and granted the new organization substantial fiscal automomy. The architects of the reconstituted mail agency hoped to make postal management more "businesslike" by giving postal executives far greater autonomy in controlling the organization's affairs. Save for the creation of the Department of Defense in 1949, it is difficult to think of other changes in the executive branch of government that have been more comprehensive.

The Postal Service is also a monument to misplaced hopes and frustrated expectations, a popular symbol of "inefficient" government service. Despite the magnitude of the changes introduced in 1971—changes that went well beyond what many persons thought were possible—the management of the mail delivery system continues to be the target of much public criticism. Citizens complain about slow delivery, mangled packages, postal workers who appear to be loafing on the job, the cost of postage, and the like. They are not new complaints; these and assorted other criticisms have been made of the postal system since long before the reorganization. Moreover, the Postal Service is certainly not the only government agency whose activities engender popular dissatisfaction.

But the mail service's troubles with the public remain especially conspicuous. One reason is that it is unlike the many agencies whose "products" are largely unseen, whose performances are not

easily monitored, and whose effects on the public are largely un-
noticed. The Postal Service's performance is always and everywhere under scrutiny, its inefficiencies and failings readily apparent. People *know* whether their mail comes late or whether the
vase sent by Aunt Eleanor arrives in pieces. Besides being able to
observe the regular performance of the postal system, citizens also
find it easy to monitor the *costs* of their mail service. That is, unlike
most government services, mail delivery is purchased by individuals, as needed, at retail counters through simple business transactions. The individual mailer, and not the general taxpayer, shoulders the bulk of the costs. This means that citizens are aware of
postal expenses (or at least, of increases in postage prices) in a way
that they are not particularly alert when it comes to their increased
tax outlays for the activities of, say, the Federal Trade Commission
or the Office for Civil Rights.

A second reason for the Postal Service's unusual susceptibility to
public criticism is that it is not difficult for the public to understand
its activities. Although some people may well be mystified that the
postal system can rapidly transfer millions of pieces of mail each
day between millions of discrete locations, even that marvel does
not induce the same public goodwill, respect, or willing suspension
of criticism accorded the public agencies that deal with highly
technical bodies of knowledge and use esoteric jargon and formulas.

Many government agencies, for example the National Institutes
of Health or the National Aeronautics and Space Administration,
perform complicated tasks that are not only generally closed to the
public's routine observation but outside the general public's realm
of understanding. Thus, even if these agencies have been exces-
sively wasteful or inefficient in, say, discovering a cure for a conta-
gious disease or shooting a man to the moon, the public will probably not know. But citizens *are* aware, sometimes painfully, of the
postal system's having smashed a package or delayed an important
letter, and they are apt to feel frustrated that a government can
send a man into space and return him in one piece but not deliver a
vase across the country intact.

Citizens who see the government accomplish highly technical
missions in less than a decade, like the moon landing, may have
trouble in understanding why a postal organization that has been
operating for nearly two centuries is not a more finely tuned instrument. This is all the more confounding since the mail operation

seems reasonably straightforward: a raw material (mail) moves through successive processing stages and emerges as a product (mail items sorted to individual addresses), delivery of which is provided as a service to the sender who has paid a fee (postage). To the average citizen, these processes appear to differ only in kind from industrial processes in many private-sector businesses and appear to be much easier than most tasks undertaken by government. The mail system does not rival space exploration or national defense in its technical complexity. It does not involve the problem, common in government, of trying to attain a goal for which there simply is no known technology, such as ending urban blight, rehabilitating criminals, or curing mental illness. The Postal Service at least has a reasonably clear mission and a technology to achieve it. Delivering the mail is a businesslike operation. In principle it is noncontroversial, and in theory its performance can be measured.

Of course, the Postal Service is only one of many government agencies that have these features. For example, states and localities operate a variety of "businesslike" enterprises, from municipally owned electric companies to state-owned liquor stores. The federal government also owns and manages various economic enterprises. For example, it operates (and charges for use of) the part of the St. Lawrence Seaway that is within the territorial borders of the United States. The federal government also owns and operates the Tennessee Valley Authority (TVA), which, among its many activities, generates electric power and supplies power wholesale to 160 local municipal and cooperative electric systems. Most government-owned enterprises have been successful in meeting their objectives and sustaining themselves financially. Most also are generally noncontroversial now, though the TVA and some other electricity producers generate environmental concerns.

It was the apparently successful organizational form of the TVA, one of the first large government corporations at the federal level, that postal reformers in the late 1960s hoped to imitate to solve some of the persistent problems of the nation's oldest public service—poor quality of service, high labor costs, an irrational rate structure, and growing deficits. As we shall see in coming chapters, postal reformers believed that these and other problems of the mail system derived from defects in organizational design, primarily insufficient managerial autonomy and flexibility. Hence the belief on the part of the reorganization's proponents that a better design would produce a better organization, which could control costs, provide service of high quality, charge reasonable rates, and become financially self-sustaining.

This book is an effort to explain what has happened as a result of the postal reorganization, to see what difference the extensive changes actually made. To the extent that we are disappointed with the reorganization's results, we shall want to know whether the problems stem from a continuing weakness in organizational design (that is, whether the postal reorganization was a good try that simply did not go far enough), whether the Postal Service's problems are inherent in its status as a governmental organization, or whether they are problems inherent in the organization's given tasks.

To answer these questions, the following chapters focus first on the purposes and scope of the reorganization and then on processes and problems fundamental to running this reconstituted postal business: devising internal management systems, pursuing efficiencies in processing and delivering mail, negotiating the wages and benefits of over 600,000 postal workers, determining the prices of mail services, and dealing with the challenges of new competition and a rapidly changing technological environment.

We shall see that the reorganization has allowed postal executives and managers to make many improvements in how the mail system performs. It will also become clear in what follows that of the problems remaining in the postal system, some are simply inherent in the organization's task. Managing a huge workforce to get the mail to every home and business in America six days a week is far more difficult than generating electric power, building and operating a water artery, or selling liquor. There is no reason to suppose that any organization—public or private, of whatever design—could perform this task without inviting the same measure of criticism.

We shall also see in what follows that many of the most serious problems of the postal system—its financial instability, for example—are the consequence of performing (and having for two centuries performed) this activity in a governmental (which is to say, political) setting. Like most government agencies, the Postal Service has many constituencies it must satisfy—the general public, residents of rural areas, the organization's own workforce, members of Congress who oversee its general operation, and industries that rely heavily on mail service in their operations (including magazine publishers, direct-mail advertisers, and mail-order companies). For years, Congress has heeded the varied demands of these postal interests, not excepting the re-election needs of congressmen, and has concomitantly saddled the postal system with widely varying and economically irreconcilable social and political objectives; the Postal Service is still required to meet most of these today.

These observations are instructive because they help us understand why the postal system performs as it does. They are also important because the federal government is increasingly turning to the corporate or quasi-corporate form of organization as a way of managing "routine" services, and yet we still know relatively little about how governmental organizations of this genre behave and why.

POSTAL REORGANIZATION

Chapter 1

POSTAL REORGANIZATION: SEARCH FOR MANAGERIAL AUTONOMY

The reorganizaion of the Post Office Department in 1971 was, above all else, an effort to increase the managerial autonomy of the mail agency. The architects of the reorganization believed that the mail delivery system was essentially a business operation that could be managed more efficiently and effectively if it were converted from an old-line cabinet agency to a government corporation. The department's old organizational arrangements appeared to restrict managerial flexibility, stifle innovation, discourage cost-consciousness, and cater to the demands of special interests. The reorganization plan reflected the postal reformers' belief that remedying these ills would require a "fundamental change in the anachronistic relationship between the Post Office and the rest of the government." [1]

We can place the reconstituted Postal Service in its organizational and political context if we examine the basic purposes of the reorganization, describe the controversies to which its proposal gave rise, and analyze the factors that led to such sweeping alterations in the institutional arrangements governing this important federal activity.

1

Public Management and the Absence
of Autonomy

The limitations on managerial autonomy in the old Post Office Department were not, of course, unique to the mail agency. Most government agencies operate with limitations on their operating
authority and managerial flexibility. The full scope of these constraints becomes most evident when one compares the managerial
environments of government agencies and private business firms.
They are worlds apart.

Perhaps the most important difference is that managers and executives in government agencies have far less control over their
organization's activities than their counterparts in private firms do.
This is not to say that managers in the private sector always enjoy
absolute autonomy. After all, they face certain constraints imposed
by the marketplace, by the demands of stockholders, by the board
of directors, and increasingly by the government. Even so, private-
sector managers generally have greater discretion over policy decisions and everyday operations than their government counterparts.
But the differences go well beyond that.

One important distinguishing characteristic between public and
private management is the source of organizational goals. The goals
of a private firm are set by its executives and board of directors. But
government agencies' goals are set by somebody outside the organization, usually a legislative body, but also pressure groups, other
agencies, the courts, a chief executive, or even the news media. This
is a serious source of frustration for public executives, particularly
those who previously held top positions in private business. Roy L.
Ash, the former head of Litton Industries, who served under presidents Nixon and Ford as director of the Office of Management and
Budget, explained the frustration this way: "Just imagine yourself as
chief executive officer where your board of directors is made up of
your employers, customers, suppliers, and competitors." [2]

Partly as a consequence of this external source of organizational
objectives, the goals in public agencies are more likely to be numerous and conflicting. These goals are also more likely than the goals
of business firms to be unrealistic and vague. Moreover, for many
government agencies, the goals are non-operational (that is, there is

no clear way of measuring progress toward attainment or even of knowing for sure when they have been achieved). Some agencies have operational goals but no feasible or possible way of attaining them—that is, the appropriate "technology" simply does not exist.

On these dimensions, some agencies and programs are in better position than others. The Social Security Administration, for example, has a clear operational goal of making prompt payment to beneficiaries, and it has the technology available to achieve that goal—high-speed computers that maintain records and print checks. Similarly, in the 1960s the National Aeronautics and Space Administration had the goal of landing a human on the moon, and it had (or was able to develop) the technological means of doing so. The Soil Conservation Service knows what it must do to prevent soil erosion, and the Department of Agriculture has ways of increasing the yield of corn crops.

But many government agencies are given goals that have no apparent available technology for attainment. There is, for example, no unambiguous and agreed-on way for government bureaucracies to achieve goals such as solving urban blight, rehabilitating prisoners, curing cancer, or stimulating the work ethic to keep people off welfare. Some agencies are in the unenviable position of having neither a technology nor a clear goal. It is not at all apparent, for example, precisely how the State Department should conduct its political negotiation with the representatives of foreign governments so as to protect and enhance U.S. interests, whatever they might be.

Public managers operate under a wide variety of other substantial constraints besides the problems of setting and attaining goals. The management in a government agency ordinarily cannot unilaterally alter the organization's factors of production—inputs such as personnel, land, buildings, and capital. For example, the various rigidities of the civil service system mean that a government agency has much less flexibility than private firms in hiring and firing employees. Moreover, a government agency cannot pay any of its employees more or less than the amount set by the legislature or by other persons outside the organization. The government agency's purchase of goods and services must be authorized and paid for by appropriated funds. Its earnings (if there are any) may not be retained by the organization. A government agency must produce statements specifying the likely environmental effects of its activi-

ties, whether building a big dam or a small post office, constructing
a large port or widening a small road. Moreover, an agency is expected to conduct most of its business in public and is thus subject
to far greater visibility and scrutiny than a private business firm is.
Along with this enhanced visibility come not only increased public
sensitivity to the agency's fiscal integrity but also heightened public
expectations that the agency will be responsive, accountable, equitable, and efficient.[3]

All these expectations mean that government agencies operate in
a much more volatile environment than business organizations do.
Outside groups affected by the agency's actions will use the political process to try to bring the agency's goals and activities in line
with their own interests and expectations. And since the agency is
likely to have more than one public to which it must pay attention,
the possibly contrary demands of those groups will only further
confuse the cross-signals the agency receives about the way it
should behave. Business firms typically operate in a less complex
environment; external demands are made known to the firm
through the working of the marketplace, as consumers exercise economic choice.

In sum, management is a more complex process (if not always
more difficult) in government agencies than in business organizations. Public managers have far less independence and discretion in
setting goals and in planning. The goals, given to the agency by
political institutions (legislatures, courts, chief executives), are not
likely to be specified clearly and are likely to be multiple and possibly irreconcilable. Planning is much more difficult in public organizations, moreover, because resources and the use of these resources are determined by political institutions whose support for
the agency is likely to be, as James Q. Wilson has suggested, contingent and conditional:[4]

> [Support] *is contingent in that it may be withdrawn, altered, or re-*
> *duced at any time, often without recourse or appeal (a bureau chief*
> *cannot sue a budget examiner or an appropriations committee chair-*
> *man for breach of contract). It is conditional in that obtaining it at all*
> *requires the executive to accept a long and growing list of constraints*
> *on his authority—civil service rules governing the hiring, assigning,*
> *and firing of personnel, accounting rules governing the uses to which*
> *money may be put, freedom of information laws designed to mini-*
> *mize his opportunities for acting in secret or maintaining confidential*
> *records, and so on.*

Though all government agencies operate under these constraints to one extent or another, agencies vary a great deal in the specific limitations to which they are subject in their everyday operations and in the amount of autonomy they possess over policy decisions within their substantive areas. For example, an agency's ability to act independently of institutions that have the authority to constrain it may be affected by the agency's functions and the expertise required for their performance. Technical knowledge and monopolized information can confer some autonomy on an agency by placing at a relative disadvantage other political elites who may lack the independent ability to verify or discredit the information the agency uses to support its policy position.[5] For instance, agencies staffed with scientists, physicians, or other prestige professionals may enjoy enhanced independence because others are willing to defer to their knowledge and expertise.

Another factor that may affect the autonomy of an agency is its formal legal status in the government. The so-called independent agencies established outside the jurisdiction of the cabinet departments (the National Science Foundation and the Railroad Retirement Board are examples) are more autonomous partly because they report directly to the President and are thus free of whatever constraints subordination to a departmental secretary would generate. As the generic name suggests, these agencies, moreover, are deliberately designed to be more independent of other political institutions and forces than cabinet agencies or bureaus are. For example, most of the independent commissions that regulate various private-sector processes or products have been vested by Congress with institutional safeguards intended to insulate them from presidential manipulation.

Perhaps the most autonomous of all federal government agencies are those with the formal legal status of government corporations. Most of these organizations occupy an area in which the distinction between governmental and business activities becomes hazy. Government corporations typically are established to isolate the management of a government-owned economic enterprise from untoward political influences. Theoretically freed of the direct control of political institutions (especially Congress), government corporations are expected to use efficient, businesslike procedures in carrying out their chartered activities.

Though most government corporations vary in the range of their specific powers, they are somewhat like private corporations in structure and operation. They usually are headed by a board of directors. The statutory charters of public corporations typically allow them much greater managerial autonomy over day-to-day operations than what is usual for traditional agencies. The corporations usually have separate personnel systems of their own, for example, and are thus exempted from all the civil service pay and employment restrictions. The corporations are permitted to set their own employment policies and to engage in direct collective bargaining with their employees over wages, working conditions, and the like. Unlike traditional government agencies or bureaus, government corporations also typically have power, acting in their own names, to sue and be sued, and to acquire, develop, and dispose of real estate and other kinds of property.

One of the most striking (and in the long run, most important) differences between government corporations and traditional agencies is in financing. Government agencies are provided with funds through annual congressional appropriations; these are frequently accompanied by greatly detailed specifications about the purposes and methods of expenditure. If an agency has any surplus funds at the end of the fiscal year, that surplus reverts to the Treasury, and funds for the next fiscal year come through another appropriation. The annual legislative review of agency activities that is part of this appropriations process theoretically forces an agency to justify its programs and budget requests and in principle keeps fiscal control of governmental activities with the people's representatives. Government corporations, by contrast, are freed of this need to win congressional approval of their budgets and program proposals, since they generally are empowered to derive their funds from their own revenues which typically come from user charges but may also come from money borrowed from the Treasury or from public bonds. This fiscal autonomy generally carries a price of sorts, in that government corporations, unlike traditional agencies, generally are expected to be financially self-sustaining. Some government corporations regularly fall short of this goal. The Commodity Credit Corporation, for example, incurs substantial annual losses in its price support program. But for most corporate organizations in government, breaking even financially remains an important goal, perhaps the ultimate one.[6]

All these characteristics, and perhaps others, make government corporations particularly attractive organizational forms for managing and operating government-owned economic enterprises. Since they are generally free of the traditional legislative restrictions on employment practices, internal decisions, and financing, government corporations have, at least theoretically, the kind of managerial flexibility needed by the government in performing certain kinds of activities efficiently and effectively. Thus, ever since World War I (especially since the 1930s), the federal government has increasingly used the corporate form of organization to manage a host of businesslike enterprises. Examples include maintaining balanced and adequate supplies of agricultural commodities and products (Commodity Credit Corporation); providing insurance coverage for bank deposits (Federal Deposit Insurance Corporation); producing electric power (Tennessee Valley Authority); maintaining industrial operations in prisons and providing goods and services for sale to federal agencies (Federal Prison Industries, Inc.); developing, operating and maintaining an effective water artery for maritime commerce (Saint Lawrence Seaway Development Corporation); and guaranteeing basic pension benefits in the event that covered plans terminate with insufficient assets (Pension Benefit Guaranty Corporation). In recent decades, state and local governments have also widely used the corporate form of organization for carrying out economic activities under public auspices. Public authorities build and operate bridges, tunnels, dams, airports, public buildings, water ports, and parks. Public authorities also have been established in many places to provide essential services: gas, water, electric power, transportation, and the like. In all these and similar operations, governments have adopted the corporate form of organization, since managerial autonomy and flexibility are considered necessary for efficient and effective operation.

At the federal level, the general criteria for using government corporations were most clearly enunciated by President Harry Truman in his 1948 budget message. Truman stated:[7]

Experience indicates that the corporate form of organization is peculiarly adapted to the administration of government programs which are predominantly of a commercial character—those which are revenue producing, are at least potentially self-sustaining, and involve a large number of business-type transactions with the public. In their business operations, such programs require greater flexibility than the customary type of appropriation budget ordinarily permits. As a rule the usefulness of a corporation lies in its ability to deal with the public in the manner employed by private enterprise for similar work.

A Postal Corporation

From this brief review, it may at first seem curious that the federal government was so late in adopting the corporate form for the oldest and largest of the nation's public businesses—the postal system. The delay is less surprising when one considers the basic reason for it; the most powerful of the Post Office Department's constituency groups—the postal employee unions and the heavy users of particular mail classes—benefited from the traditional institutional arrangements governing the postal system. The postal employee unions substantially influenced Congress on all postal matters and were particularly successful at keeping postal wages on a par with wages paid in highly unionized private-sector industries. Similarly, the industries for which mail service is a particularly important factor in operating—especially magazine and newspaper publishing and direct-mail advertising—also had substantial influence on Congress; they were successful over the years in securing indirect federal subsidies for their operations by persuading legislators to keep postal rates low, making up any postal deficits through larger appropriations rather than through rate hikes.

In short, these influential groups in the Post Office Department's environment had an obvious interest in preserving the institutional and political arrangements that enabled them to shape postal policies to their liking. Against this constellation of interests, early proposals to convert the Post Office Department to a government corporation (such as the plan the first Hoover Commission advanced in 1949) went nowhere.[8]

But by the late 1960s, circumstances in the postal policy arena had changed in numerous ways, so that a proposal to create a postal corporation was no longer necessarily doomed to defeat.

First, by the mid-1960s, the problems in postal operations were considered increasingly critical. Congress had for years been pinching pennies when it came to appropriating funds to the Post Office Department for research and development; Congress preferred instead to use available money for keeping wages up and postal rates down. Consequently, mail was still being handled and sorted with much the same facilities and equipment that had been used for decades, even though the torrent of mail pouring through the postal system was swelling by roughly 2 billion pieces annually; the amount increased from 28 billion pieces in 1940 to 78 billion in 1967.[9]

It was probably inevitable that the cumulative stress of burgeoning mail volumes and retarded industrial development would someday cripple the system or a major part of it. In October 1966, Chicago's massive main post office—at 13 stories and 60 acres of workspace, one of the largest postal facilities in the world—broke down. For three weeks the facility was paralyzed by a backlog of mail exceeding 10 million pieces. Railroad cars and trailer trucks full of mail choked approaches to the post office, complicating the efforts of rattled Washington officials to divert to other cities much of the mail usually processed in Chicago.[10] Close observers of the postal system's condition in the 1960s had long recognized that its inadequacies and accumulating stresses portended chaos. But it took this highly visible breakdown in the system to alert the public and its political institutions to the agency's problems and to stimulate sweeping changes in postal agency management.

The everyday mail operations were not the only feature of the postal system that generated concern among politicians and others conversant with postal policy; the mail agency also seemed to be facing a deepening financial crisis. Productivity was unimpressive, the workforce was growing rapidly, and labor costs were becoming a rapidly increasing percentage of the total postal operating budget. The operating deficit nearly doubled in the three years between 1964 ($651.7 million) and 1967 ($1.1 billion).[11]

Another factor besides the apparently worsening condition of postal operations and fiscal affairs was favorable to a postal corporation proposal in the late 1960s. It was the decreasing political utility of postal matters to most congressmen, except those in leadership positions on the post office committees. Apart from, say, the occasional chance to fight for keeping a small community post office, the postal system offered congressmen little in the way of opportunities for enhancing their own reelection chances. Even the long-standing patronage attractions of the postal system had lost their appeal for legislators, who had learned over time that the chance to appoint a local postmaster as often as not turned into a political liability for the legislator, since disappointed office seekers far outnumbered the one lucky job recipient.

By the late 1960s, moreover, Congress and the President were less reluctant than they had been in the past to relinquish control over postal affairs. There were too many other things increasingly demanding the attention of these political elites—the war in Vietnam, urban disorders, and rising health-care costs, to cite only a few of the urgent items then on the federal government's agenda. The Postal Service's relatively prosaic mission did not exactly accord it an attractive position on the changing political agenda—especially if the worsening condition of the mail agency might reflect badly on elected officials.

Finally, the postal corporation idea gained substantial currency in the late 1960s because this time it had the support of an unusually determined proponent—the Post Office Department itself. In many ways, this would prove to be the most important factor in the push for reconstituting the organization of the postal system.

Initial Impetus for Change

In 1966, when President Lyndon Johnson first appointed his special assistant for congressional relations, Lawrence F. O'Brien, to become postmaster general, persons who cared about the postal system's problems despaired. The appointment appeared to be in line with the long-standing presidential practice of giving the top job to a trusted political ally who could serve the President as a kind of minister without portfolio, dealing with a wide range of matters not related to postal affairs. As a result of this traditional practice, the postmaster general's chair had seldom been occupied by persons who were at once concerned about increasing the effectiveness of postal management and skilled at such a job. But O'Brien surprised those who worried about his appointment, because he committed himself early to a serious effort at managing the postal system. The former presidential aide recognized that if he could substantially reverse the deteriorating performance of the mail agency, his own reputation, already glowing, would take on added luster.[12]

O'Brien had been in office only a few months in 1966 before he fully appreciated what a hard task he had set for himself. The complex and anomalous postal rate-making procedures, the backwardness of postal facilities and equipment, the restrictions of the budgetary process, and the inflexibility of the civil service system all startled O'Brien by their apparent intractability. The new postmaster general began to regard as futile any attempt to make isolated improvements.

, For O'Brien, the most frustrating problem of all was the limited autonomy he had in trying to manage the mail agency. Although he was the head of the largest civilian agency in the government, with over 700,000 employees scattered in more than 40,000 facilities throughout the country, he had, as he complained to members of a congressional subcommittee in 1967, no control over the organization's revenues, no control over the employees' pay or other conditions of their employment, no control over the kinds or levels of service the organization provided, no control over the system's physical facilities, and at best only limited control over the transportation methods the organization used.[13]

In short, O'Brien faced the same situation confronting most other political executives in Washington; control over important elements of his agency's activities was distributed among other organizations and institutions—the White House, Congress, the Civil Service Commission, the General Services Administration, the General Accounting Office, the Treasury Department, and in this case the Interstate Commerce Commission and the Civil Aeronautics Board also. In O'Brien's view, subjecting postal policy to this fragmentation and dispersion of control was absurd. He believed the postal service was essentially a business operation that could be managed much more efficiently and effectively if its executives had greater managerial autonomy—that is, independent control of the organization's finances, personnel policies, service levels, and the like.

O'Brien was finally moved to try for drastic changes in the organizational and political status of the Post Office Department. Accordingly, he created a small, highly confidential task force inside the Post Office Department and charged it with developing a reform plan that would provide postal management with much greater autonomy in its policymaking.[14]

Early in 1967, the task force brought O'Brien what he wanted—a proposal for converting the Post Office Department into a more businesslike, corporate form of organization.[15] And in April 1967, the postmaster general stunned an audience at a Washington convention of the Magazine Publishers Association by proposing that the Post Office Department be removed from the President's cabinet and converted to a government corporation. O'Brien referred in his speech to the "restrictive jungle of legislation and custom" that had grown up around the Post Office Department over the years, leaving postal management almost "no control" over the system. O'Brien told his audience: "The only effective action I foresee is sweeping it away entirely."[16]

The speech delighted members of the business community, who saw in O'Brien's proposal an acknowledgment of the effectiveness of private-business management techniques. And within a week of the address, President Johnson further sought to solidify the support of businessmen for the idea when he chartered the President's Commission on Postal Organization to study the proposal. The President selected Frederick R. Kappel, the retired board chairman of the American Telephone and Telegraph Company, to head the commission, whose members could have made up a roll call of American business elite. They included George P. Baker, dean of the Harvard Business School; David E. Bell, vice president of the Ford Foundation; Fred J. Borch, president of the General Electric Company; David Ginsburg, a partner in Ginsburg and Feldman; J. Irwin Miller, chairman of the board of the Cummins Engine Company; W. Beverly Murphy, president of the Campbell Soup Company; and Ralph A. Peterson, president of the Bank of America. George Meany, president of the AFL-CIO, was also included on the commission as a token nod to the postal labor unions, whose support for a change to a business-minded postal corporation was unlikely anyway.

The commission, in approaching its task, decided to assemble a small professional staff and to engage some of the nation's top management consulting firms for the development of basic information and analysis.[17] The consultants produced a collection of nostrums supporting the conversion of the postal system to a corporate form of organization. One student of government corporations has suggested that this is the pattern to be expected whenever management consultants are called in to make recommendations on organizational structure:[18]

> *Public corporations are one of the most common forms of new organization recommended to governments by management consultants today. Tailoring their advice to the pragmatic needs of their political clients and usually passing on the orthodox views of the public authority with little fresh analysis, consultants yield to the appealing temptation to solve each new public policy problem by establishing a new institution and giving it a free hand, unencumbered by the persistent conflicts, the biases, and the historical stalemates of existing*

> *government agencies. . . . A common script—define a specialized problem, seek a purely organizational solution, spin off a government corporation—unfolds repeatedly with different actors and settings. The Connecticut Resources Recovery Authority and the U.S Postal Service are examples.*

And in fact, the general contractor's report to the commission did read like a formulary of organizational management principles. The consultants from Arthur D. Little, Inc., noting that certain dominant principles of organizational and managerial thought in the United States had strongly influenced their concepts of what is "natural, obvious, inevitable, and proper in organizational behavior," recorded some of those principles:[19]

> *An organization is a container which must hold all essential elements and no superfluous ones. Its boundaries are the key to its manageability. Such functions as budgeting and labor relations, for example, must not spill out of the container, and such elements as patronage politics shold not wash into it.*

The consultants found that the organization and management of the Post Office Department conformed ·not to this "contained" mode of organization but to a "fragmented," or "politically oriented," design with different characteristics:[20]

> *This organization does not have all its elements in one managerial container. It occupies ground which is simultaneously occupied by other systems and is itself an aspect of a larger system. . . . A fragmented organization is designed to reduce the need for reliance on top-level authority. Its many bits of limited discretion, limited authority, limited mobility, limited opportunity, limited incentive and limited responsibility are controlled by highly specific and comprehensive legislative prescriptions built into rule books, procedural manuals and administrative directives. . . . It progresses by means of incremental improvisation, as opposed to sweeping systemic design. Coalitions have to be built and rebuilt to support each bargained "set" of incremental changes.*

Though the Arthur D. Little, Inc., consultants acknowledged that both kinds of organization and management—the contained mode and the fragmented, politically oriented mode—are "rational, effective, and legitimate approaches in our society," they clearly saw the businesslike boundaries of a contained organization as the more promising organizational form for the Post Office.[21] The other consultants' studies also substantiated Postmaster General O'Brien's proposal of a government corporation for handling the mail.

In June 1968, the President's Commission on Postal Organization issued its report, identifying in clear terms what it considered the fundamental problem of the postal system:[22]

> *The organization of the Post Office as an ordinary Cabinet depart-
> ment guarantees that* the nominal managers of the postal service do
> not have the authority to run the postal service. *The important man-
> agement decisions of the Post Office are beyond their control and
> therefore cannot be made on the basis of business judgment.*

Accordingly, the commission formally recommended creating a postal corporation with full management responsibility and authority vested in a board of directors that would select the postmaster general. The corporation would have the power to sue and be sued, settle claims, enter its own contracts, acquire property, construct and operate its own facilities, issue revenue bonds, adopt rules and regulations, and determine its own system of accounts. It would have its own merit system independent of the federal civil service, and it would negotiate directly with the postal unions over pay, related benefits, and other conditions of employment. The corporation's board of directors would establish postal rates (subject to veto by concurrent resolution of Congress) after hearings by an internal panel of rate commissioners.[23]

The Kappel commission's report received widespread support from the press;[24] but as frequently happens with the recommendations of presidential study panels, no action was taken on the proposals for almost a year.[25] Besides the usual delays in formulating policy and the difficulties of assembling a supporting coalition for such an extensive proposal, further delay arose when the reform impetus cooled temporarily; this happened because President Johnson had removed himself from the 1968 presidential election race and Postmaster General O'Brien had relinquished his post to work on the presidential campaign of Senator Robert F. Kennedy. Thus not until early 1969, with the inauguration of President Richard M. Nixon, were efforts to build a coalition in support of the proposal rekindled. President Nixon and his postmaster general, Winton M. Blount, a successful Alabama contractor and former chairman of the U.S. Chamber of Commerce, indicated early in 1969 that they were committed to reorganization. Under the Nixon-Blount administration, the Post Office Department launched an intense and skillful campaign for the agency's overhaul, joining the legislative battle.

Labor and Business Take Sides

Not surprisingly, the sweeping reorganization proposal elicited both strong opposition and firm support from various corners of the postal policy arena. The most powerful and concentrated opposition came from the postal employee unions. These groups vigorously opposed any serious changes in postal policy, fearing a sharp reduction in their influence if the role of Congress in making postal policy were curtailed. The unions had great influence on Capitol Hill and had been very successful in achieving their goals through legislation. They feared that the proposed change to direct collective bargaining would work to the political and economic disadvantage of postal workers, especially since the reorganization proposal retained the prohibition on strikes by postal workers.

A popular objection voiced by the unions was that the reorganization would vest too much power in an isolated, independent authority in which narrow considerations of economy and efficiency would guide managerial decisions. Under a corporate postal system, the unions argued, there would be no way of ensuring that the actions of postal management would respond to public interests and needs (not to mention the interests and needs of the unions).[26] Moreover, although the postal workers' organizations recognized that certain reforms were undoubtedly desirable and necessary, they insisted that the wholesale revisions sought through the reorganization might prove to be a remedy worse than the problem. One union spokesman told those present at a congressional hearing: "The Post Office must be reformed, but it must be reformed in a prudent way. There are better ways of ridding a dog of fleas than drowning the dog."[27]

The opposition of these employee groups was a formidable obstacle to the passage of the reorganization plan. The unions, which were well financed and unusually skillful at the art of lobbying, commanded respect and attention on Capitol Hill. Moreover, the permeability of the policymaking process in the federal government (allowing numerous points of intervention for interested groups) provided the reorganization's opponents with many opportunities to block action on the measure.

But the supporters of reorganization were also in a strong position. The time was ripe for a significant change in the management of the postal system. And the coalition in support of the reorganization proposal was led by the Post Office Department itself, with the full support and encouragement of the Nixon White House. The principal allies of the executive branch in this reorganization were the general business community, the large publishers, and some strong and well-placed members of Congress (such as Representative Morris K. Udall, Democrat from Arizona) who believed the plan had merit.[28]

The business community, which is the source of 80 per cent of total mail volume, favored the proposal in the belief that improvements in service and efficiency would accrue to the postal system if management tools that private enterprise had found useful were applied. To the business community, it only made sense that, as a spokesman for the National Association of Manufacturers put it, "our society should employ the know-how developed in our commercial and industrial life to manage this function that so closely resembles a commercial or industrial enterprise." [29] The reorganization seemed to hold the promise of improved service, lowered costs, and steadier rates. It was this last prospect that chiefly accounted for the support of the large publishers. For example, Stephen E. Kelly, the president of the Magazine Publishers Association, told a House committee considering the reorganization plan:[30]

> In addition to the higher postage costs resulting from eight legislated increases by the Congress in the past 11 years, this frequent recurrence of rate bills . . . keeps the industry constantly off balance in long-range planning.
>
> Magazines have encouraged the long-term subscription—2, 3, 5 years. These rates cannot be changed without substantial lead time. Magazines are locked into them, at a minimum usually, for 18 months. Increases in postal rates simply cannot be passed along speedily to any of our customers—readers or advertisers. And, as an industry, we do not have the profits to absorb them. . . . The Post Office is the major mode of distribution for magazines. We have, therefore, an enlightened self-interest in proposals to reorganize the Post Office as well as a commitment to our reading public to support sound programs that strengthen and improve service, at reasonable cost.

Postal Officials Engineer Reorganization

When top postal officials began in 1969 to map a strategy to secure passage of the reorganization plan, they anticipated several hurdles. First was the potential reluctance of congressmen, especially members of the House Post Office and Civil Service Committee, to relinquish the control they exercised over the Post Office, or to lose the attentions of the powerful postal unions. Second, postal officials worried about generating sufficient public support for the reorganization, especially since the proposed changes held no promise of immediate benefits and could even appear threatening to services the public expected. Third was the opposition of the department's own rank-and-file employees. The unions' resistance to the plan loomed as perhaps the most formidable obstacle.

Thus, the Post Office Department's top officials set about trying to quiet the anxieties of these various constituencies and to find ways of reducing resistance and building a solid coalition in support of the reorganization. In early 1969, Postmaster General Winton Blount assembled a team of high-level postal executives whose collective task was to smooth the path for postal reorganization legislation.

This group developed an intricate "marketing plan," the ultimate objective of which was to win the support of enough representatives and senators to ensure that the measure was passed in Congress. The reorganization strategists operated on the assumption that congressmen were most responsive to three things:[31]

1. The expressed desires and demands of their constituents.
2. The position taken by leading makers of public opinion (for example, newspapers, television, and local leaders).
3. The views of special-interest groups and large voting blocs.

To help sell the proposal to skeptical members of Congress, the Congressional Liaison Office in the Post Office Department enlisted the efforts of large corporations and trade associations. Some of these organizations lent lobbyists to the Post Office to aid in the effort. Among the organizations that helped the Post Office to lobby reluctant congressmen in 1969 were Sears, Roebuck, and General Electric, Procter and Gamble, J. C. Penney, the Chamber of Commerce, the Magazine Publishers Association, the American Retail Federation, and the American Farm Bureau Federation.[32]

But postal officials recognized that even this lobbying blitz might not be enough. As one reorganization strategist in the Post Office Department put it in a memo to his colleagues:[33]

It should be accepted that a massive selling job will be required for any plan that will result in Congress relinquishing control over the

> *bulk of postal operations. By law we are debarred from this kind of selling job, although of course the public pronouncements of the Post-master General do not fall within that limitation. [United States Code, Title 18, Sec. 1913, prohibits an agency from lobbying Congress with appropriated funds.] We can, however, try to engineer some form of separate organization designed to further improving postal service. Perhaps the U.S. Chamber of Commerce might designate this as "improved postal service year" and provide an ongoing organization to press for reform; or, failing that, a foundation might be enlisted to establish a working group for reorganization.*

Postal management's strategy here was not entirely unusual. Indeed, as students of public bureaucracies have noted, executive agencies—in their efforts to mobilize political support for programs they administer or changes they wish to make—have become skilled at creating and organizing pressures to which they seem to be responding. As Francis E. Rourke has suggested:[34]

> *The organization of such apparent pressure group activity thus provides a means by which these agencies can conceal their own central role in the policy process. The initiative appears to be with outside organizations, but the activities of these external groups are actually instigated by the agency itself.*

In a process akin to this, the Post Office Department supplemented its own internally directed push for a postal reorganization by sanctioning and helping to establish an organization known as Citizens Committee for Postal Reform (CCPR). Headed by former Postmaster General Larry O'Brien and former U.S. Senator Thruston B. Morton, CCPR had the financial backing of some of the nation's largest business firms. The committee was the nation's seventeenth largest lobbyist in 1969, and the tenth largest in 1970.[35] Among its chief backers were McGraw-Hill, Inc., Sears, Roebuck and Company, the Bank of America, Montgomery Ward, General Foods, Pitney-Bowes, Time, Inc., and Standard Oil of New Jersey.[36] Included among the organization's stated objectives were these:[37]

> *To elevate this proposal [reorganization] to the status of a major domestic issue and request each presidential and congressional candidate to take a stand favoring creation of the postal corporation.*
>
> *To develop broad-based support for the postal corporation among the American people through education and information programs.*
>
> *To assist in convincing those postal employees, postal unions, mail users, leaders in government, and people who are not presently convinced, that the postal corporation is in their best interest and should be strongly supported.*

The efforts of CCPR to achieve these goals were part of a larger strategy directed by the Post Office Department to build support for the reorganization. Relying in part on the aid of CCPR, Post Office strategists ran supportive advertisements in newspapers and arranged for a continuous flow of general news and feature stories in the mass media. They also launched a campaign to flood newspaper editors with letters expressing support for the reorganization, distributed brochures to voluntary associations and schools, arranged for the postmaster general to appear on national and regional television and radio programs, and formed a national speakers' bureau with branch operations in each region to make speakers available for public functions, including convention panels, Rotary Club meetings, and the like. The list of such activities is a long one.[38]

In these pitches to the public, the reorganization's advocates repeatedly portrayed a postal system on the verge of collapse and claimed that the best way to save it was to "take politics out of the system" and infuse it with private business management techniques. The implication was clear; postal reform would bring faster and more reliable service, would reduce the postal deficit that burdened the taxpayer, and would slow the rise in postage rates.

In its appeals to members of Congress for support, the Post Office Department sought to persuade the legislators that they had an obligation to provide the public with a revitalized postal system. The department tried to convince the legislators that postal reform was what the voters wanted and that support of the reorganization measure would be to the members' advantage when they were campaigning for reelection.[39] The reorganization's advocates also tried to persuade the legislators of other advantages they would reap from the reorganization: they would no longer be bothered by postal job seekers, pressed by the unions for wage increases and improved benefits, pestered by the special mailers for restraints on postage rates, or flooded by constituent complaints about postal service.

In sum, the Post Office Department initiated a massive effort in 1969 and 1970 to achieve the reorganization that seemed to hold the promise of managerial autonomy. As time passed, the groups that proved most resistant to the department's active solicitations for support were the labor unions representing the department's own rank-and-file employees. As already indicated, the unions were not convinced that the reorganization held any advantages for them or their members. Equally important, the unions believed that the whole question of reorganization was obscuring an issue they felt merited more immediate attention—a pay raise for postal workers.

The Pay Issue Takes Precedence

Early in 1969, at the same time the Post Office Department was preparing the initial drafts of the reorganization bill, the postal labor unions were starting to push for a wage increase. On February 12, 1969, the Nixon Administration revealed its intention of increasing postal pay by just under 3 per cent. The postal unions argued for a more substantial increase, and after some prodding the Administration offered to raise the increase to just over 4 per cent.[40] The unions still were dissatisfied, so they turned to Congress for help.

On Capitol Hill, the subject of postal pay quickly overshadowed the postal reorganization legislation and continued to do so throughout the remainder of 1969. In October the House overwhelmingly approved a postal pay bill that provided for an 11 per cent pay increase. But by Thanksgiving neither house of Congress yet had taken substantial action on the reorganization measure. The Post Office Department, fearing that the chances for passage of the reorganization might fade if action on it were delayed too long, sought to use the pay issue as leverage to gain support from the unions for the reorganization package.[41] The President became involved in the process, and the parties began in earnest to negotiate a settlement on a combination pay package and reorganization plan. Despite apparent breakthroughs in December, the year ended with no progress on either measure.[42]

The new year began with still no break in the impasse. The Nixon Administration was willing and able to withhold action on the pay raise until it won some measure of support from the unions for the reorganization proposal. The unions, on the other hand, had virtual veto power over any reorganization legislation, and they could be counted on to exercise it until their pay demands were met. When this stalemate persisted into February 1970, rank-and-file postal workers began to talk of a postal strike.

The department acted quickly to try to stem the growing discontent of postal workers and to save the reorganization proposal. Post

Office Department General Counsel David Nelson, along with John Gabusi, a staff member of a House postal subcommittee, drafted a substitute reorganization proposal providing for an 11 per cent pay increase retroactive to January 1, 1970. The House Post Office and Civil Service Committee approved and reported the bill on March 12, 1970. The bill also drew the support of the powerful National Association of Letter Carriers. But all the accompanying rhetoric about the new measure being "an important first step," and "a workable bill," did not convince militant postal workers. On March 18, 1970, postal workers in New York City went on a strike that spread throughout the nation and lasted for eight days—crippling business activities and severely disrupting commerce.[43]

With workers still out on strike on March 24, the leaders of the main postal unions seemed to worsen the prospects of settlement when they announced that they would no longer even consider a pay raise tied to a postal reorganization proposal. When Labor Secretary George Shultz, who had been called in to help solve the dispute, argued that "to link the justifiable demands of postal employees with reform, and to leave the thing pending seems to be a colossal error," Postmaster General Blount announced that the administration was willing to discuss all issues involved in the strike, and that postal reorganization would not necessarily be a prerequisite to pay legislation.[44]

The next afternoon, March 25, 1970, negotiations began in Washington between postal labor and management. The talks went on for almost a week without progress. Finally, on April 1, a compromise plan emerged. The proposal offered the unions a two-step pay increase: the first, an immediate 6 per cent increase, retroactive to December 29, 1969; the second, an 8 per cent increase contingent on union support for postal reorganization. The proposal also included an offer to have the unions participate in formulating the details of the reform plan. Both sides agreed to the compromise resolution on April 2, 1970.[45]

Further negotiations continued for two weeks in an attempt to develop a reorganization package that would have the support of the Post Office and the unions alike. On April 16 the parties finally reached an agreement on the terms of a postal reorganization proposal. The agreement included most of the same features the Post Office had been pushing all along, but there was one important change intended to secure beyond doubt the support of the unions;

the proposal provided for third-party binding arbitration—a provision the unions had sought as compensation for the reduction in Congress's role in making postal policy and the consequent severing of the unions' principal line of influence over postal labor policies. In short, the proponents of postal reorganization were able to win the support of the unions for the reorganization plan by agreeing to the 14 per cent pay increase and the binding arbitration provision.

Final Consideration and Passage

The Nixon Administration immediately transmitted the proposed legislation to congress, calling it "a measure that could ultimately lead to a cure of the problems that have been festering for years in the postal system."[46] The bill passed through the House without any important substantive changes; but it faced a more complex path in the Senate, where some important changes were made in the new postal rate-making machinery. The final bill reported by the conference committee included no more substantive changes.

On the afternoon that the House took the final legislative action on the bill (August 6, 1970), Postmaster General Winton Blount told reporters at a press conference:[47]

> *When we came here a year and a half ago with the Nixon Administration, nobody held out much hope for the possibility of reorganizing the Post Office Department. . . . There were strong opinions held on this matter. All of these conflicting opinions have now been brought into accommodation with the passage of the legislation. And we are happy to get that over with and to get on with the implementation of this legislation as soon as possible.*

In a ceremony held in the postmaster general's reception room on August 12, 1970, President Nixon signed the Postal Reorganization Act. Less than eleven months later, on July 1, 1971, the new United States Postal Service officially became an independent establishment of the federal government.

The Postal Reorganization Act made many important changes in the institutional and procedural arrangements for postal management. The act, among other things, did the following:

- Vested direction of the Postal Service in an eleven-member board of governors, nine members of the board being appointed by the President on a bipartisan basis with the advice and consent of the Senate. These members in turn appoint a tenth member of the board, the postmaster general, who serves as the chief executive officer of the Postal Service. These ten appoint a deputy postmaster general, who serves as the eleventh member of the board.

- Established the independent Postal Rate Commission to recommend postal rates and classifications for adoption by the board of governors.
- Established an independent personnel system for the Postal Service, with provisions for direct collective bargaining between postal management and the unions.
- Authorized appropriations for a general "public service" subsidy through fiscal year 1979 in an amount equal to 10 per cent ($920 million) of the fiscal 1971 appropriations to the Post Office Department. After 1979, this annual authorization declines by 1 per cent a year through fiscal 1984, by which time the Postal Service was expected to be self-sustaining.
- Provided for the gradual phasing out of preferential rates for certain categories of mail and required that rates for each class of mail cover those costs directly and indirectly attributable to it plus some "reasonably assignable" portion of the system's institutional costs.
- Authorized the Postal Service to borrow money and issue public bonds (up to $10 billion) to finance postal buildings and mechanization.

All these and many other provisions of the Postal Reorganization Act made the law both the most controversial and the most comprehensive postal legislation in the mail system's almost 200-year history.

Factors Conducive to Reorganization

The remarkable feature of the successful passage of the postal reorganization plan is that the proponents of this massive overhaul of the mail agency were able to overcome both the opposition of powerful and well-organized interests and the procedural bias in the American political system against those who try to reorganize the structure or redirect the activities of government. Because of the extraordinary advantages built into the political system favoring those who oppose changes, it is cause for wonder that this set of extensive changes reached enactment. But this particular reorganization (and the policy arena in which it took place) possessed several distinctive features that increased the likelihood of success for those who promoted its passage.

First, the reorganization effort did not find postal officials in the position of protective bureaucrats looking with fear on outside calls for changes in their domain. Rather, the whole postal reform movement was essentially an attempt to secure managerial autonomy—independent authority to decide about financing, personnel, services, and other basic policy matters. Thus, from the time of its earliest conception within the department itself, the reorganization plan was vigorously supported by the highest reaches of the postal bureaucracy—a prominent vantage point from which the basic outlines of the reorganization idea were drafted and coalitions built supporting it.

Second, the push for the reorganization's enactment required no enormous expenditure of political capital by any individual or organization except the Post Office Department itself (and it really had nothing to lose by its efforts). Many significant reorganization proposals fail to receive adequate political support partly because building a sufficiently strong coalition requires too great an outlay of political capital, usually by the President, with no guarantee of success.[48] But in this case President Nixon did not have to spend precious political resources, partly since there were no substantial disputes over the plan from within the executive branch (more on this below), and partly since the reorganization would disrupt congressional committee structures to only a limited extent. Moreover, proponents of the plan were able to offer members of Congress the appealing prospect of being freed from the responsibility of having to make politically uncomfortable decisions about patronage, rates, and wages. And although the reorganization plan drew some sustained opposition from the unions, it enjoyed strong support from other constituencies—large publishers and the general business community.

Third, throughout much of its legislative history, the controversial reorganization proposal was overshadowed by the even more volatile issue of a pay increase for postal employees. This concurrence of events had the dual effect of shielding the reform plan from some of the dilution that fuller scrutiny and wider debate might have brought it and of giving the measure's proponents the opportunity to enlist the support of the postal unions.

Fourth, unlike the situation facing those who might promote re-organization in, for example, federal health or education policy, the postal policy setting was relatively isolated and free-standing. That is, there were no other federal agencies charged with performing even remotely similar tasks. Thus, no agencies rose in alarm over the reorganization's potential effects on their activities—a common occurrence in policy arenas when several agencies have like missions.[49] Moreover, unlike many other federal agencies, the Post Office Department did not operate through state or local agencies or depend on them; therefore, advocates of the reorganization did not have the additional problem of having to satisfy the demands of state or local officials who might have felt threatened. Also, the postal reorganization measure did not try to elevate the organizational status of the department or its functions at the implicit expense of other federal programs.[50] Postal reformers were not threatening other programs and priorities with arguments that the increasing severity of the postal problem required that the agency receive more federal money or increased attention from the President and Congress. Rather, the postal reformers explicitly sought to remove the department from the President's cabinet, to reduce the number of tax dollars devoted to postal activities, and to decrease attention from members of Congress.

Finally, the advocates of postal reorganization had more than sterile, unemotional arguments to back their proposal. Though dull theories of organizational management provided the chief theoretical justification for the proposal, the reorganization's proponents were able to sell it to the public as a way of improving service while holding rates steady, and as a way of ridding the postal system of "politics" and everything the pejorative sense of that word conveyed—corruption, waste, favoritism, and the like. The postal reorganization's advocates, in framing the issue to the public that way, made it especially difficult for members of Congress to oppose the plan.

In short, the advocates of postal reorganization enjoyed great advantages in their efforts to surmount the usual array of obstacles confronting those who try to reform bureaucracy through reorganization. And some of these same features that lubricated the political wheels in the pre-enactment stage of the measure (especially the freedom from having to work through or with other agencies) also helped in implementing many of the reorganization's provisions.[51]

But the activities and performance of the Postal Service in the years since the reorganization indicate that even in a policy arena relatively unencumbered by ambiguous goals and administrative entanglements, achieving the intent of reorganization is difficult at best. That is, postal executives have found (as the following chapters show) that the postal system is less adaptable to business management techniques than the reformers believed, and that the managerial autonomy they thought they won through the reorganization does not extend to some important elements of postal policy.

Endnotes

1. President's Commission on Postal Organization, Report of the Commission, *Towards Postal Excellence* (Washington: U.S. Government Printing Office, 1968), p. 53.
2. Quoted in Gordon Chase, "Managing, Compared," *New York Times*, March 14, 1978, p. 35.
3. See James Q. Wilson, "The Bureaucracy Problem," *Public Interest*, no. 6 (Winter 1967), pp. 3–9.
4. James Q. Wilson, *The Investigators: Managing FBI and Narcotics Agents* (New York: Basic Books, 1978), p. 164.
5. Francis E. Rourke, *Bureaucracy, Politics, and Public Policy*, 2d ed. (Boston: Little, Brown, 1976), pp. 15, 84.
6. Harold Seidman, *Politics, Position, and Power*, 3rd ed. (New York: Oxford University Press, 1980), p. 270. In this discussion of government corporations, I have relied largely on Seidman's lucid treatment in pp. 265–276.
7. *House Document 19*, 80th Cong., pp. M57–M62, quoted in Seidman, *Politics*, p. 276.
8. See *Task Force Report on the Post Office, Appendix I*, prepared for the [Hoover] Commission on Organization of the Executive Branch of the Government, by Robert Heller and Associates (Washington: U.S. Government Printing Office, 1949).
9. United States, Post Office Department, *Annual Report of the Postmaster General, 1969* (Washington: U.S. Government Printing Office, 1970), p. 241.
10. President's Commission on Postal Organization, *Towards Postal Excellence*, p. 11. For a full description of the Chicago collapse, see Charles Remsberg, "The Day the Mails Stopped," *Saturday Review*, December 17, 1968, pp. 21–24.
11. *Annual Report of the Postmaster General, 1969*, p. 246.

12. Harold E. Dolenga, "An Analytical Case Study of the Policy Formation Process: Postal Reform and Reorganization" (Ph.D. diss., Northwestern University, 1973), pp. 235–238.

13. U.S., Congress, House, Committee on Appropriations, *Postal Appropriations, Hearings before a Subcommittee of the House Committee on Appropriations,* 90th Cong. 2d Sess., 1967, pp. 27–28.

14. Dolenga, "Postal Reform," pp. 238–240.

15. Special Task Force, "Report on Improving the Postal Service: Should the Post Office Be More Autonomous?" Confidential report presented to Postmaster General Lawrence O'Brien, Washington, March 1967.

16. Lawrence F. O'Brien, "A New Design for the Postal Service," address presented at meeting of the Magazine Publishers Association and the American Society of Magazine Editors, Washington, April 3, 1967.

17. The commission selected Arthur D. Little, Inc., as general contractor, to perform a wide-ranging study of all aspects of postal operations and management. To supplement the general contractor's report, and to provide more detailed information on certain areas of postal operations, the commission engaged three other firms—Robert R. Nathan Associates, Price Waterhouse and Company, and Foster Associates, Inc.—to conduct special studies on personnel, finance, and rates, respectively. The commission's own small staff was headed by Murray Comarow, who came to the job on temporary leave from his position as executive director of the Federal Power Commission. It coordinated and monitored the various studies, examined the findings, and drafted the report for the commission.

18. Annemarie Hauck Walsh, *The Public's Business: The Politics and Practices of Government Corporations* (Cambridge, Mass.: MIT Press, 1978), p. 48.

19. President's Commission on Postal Organization, *Towards Postal Excellence,* Annex, vol. 1, part 1, p. 122.

20. *Ibid.,* pp. 123–124.

21. *Ibid.,* p. 125.

22. President's Commission on Postal Organization, *Towards Postal Excellence,* p. 33. (Emphasis as in original.)

23. *Ibid.,* pp. 55–64.

24. See, for example, *New York Times,* July 24, 1968, p. 40; *Washington Post,* August 11, 1968, p. B6; and David Stanford, "The Post Office: Who Needs It?" *New Republic,* August 31, 1968, p. 13.

25. Research by Thomas Wolanin suggests that although governmental action in response to recommendations of presidential commissions is more frequent than is widely believed, there is still a substantial percentage of cases in which no action whatsoever is taken. See Wolanin, *Presidential Advisory Commissions* (Madison: University of Wisconsin Press, 1975), pp. 139, 193.

26. U.S., Congress, House, Committee on Post Office and Civil Service, *Post Office Reorganization, Hearings before the Committee on Post Office and Civil Service,* 91st Cong., 1st Sess., 1969, pp. 343–345, 378, 733–735, 837.

27. *Ibid.,* p. 735.

28. For a full legislative history of the postal reorganization plan, highlighting the roles of some of the sympathetic members of Congress, see Dolenga. "Postal Reform" chap. 12.

29. U.S., Congress, House, *Post Office Reorganization Hearings*, p. 705.

30. *Ibid.*, pp. 796–797.

31. U.S. Post Office Department, "Marketing Plan," internal strategy document, dated March 1, 1969, pp. 6, 7; files of the postmasters general, U.S. Postal Service, Washington.

32. Confidential internal memorandum from Post Office Department's Congressional Liaison Office to Postmaster General Winton Blount, August 27, 1969; files of the postmasters general, U.S. Postal Service, Washington.

33. Jim Henderson, memorandum to the General Counsel (David A. Nelson), "Reorganization of Postal Service, Suggestions for," dated April 7, 1969, typewritten.

34. Francis E. Rourke, *Bureaucracy, Politics, and Public Policy*, 2d ed. (Boston: Little, Brown, 1976), p. 48.

35. *Congressional Quarterly Weekly Report*, July 31, 1970, p. 1967; August 6, 1971, p. 1681.

36. U.S., Congress, House, *Post Office Reorganization, Hearings*, pp. 629–632.

37. Citizens for a Postal Corporation, Statement of Organizational Purpose, undated, typewritten. "Citizens for a Postal Corporation" was predecessor to the Citizens Committee for Postal Reform.

38. U.S. Post Office Department, "Marketing Plan," pp. 15–20, 22.

39. *Ibid.*, pp. 13, 22–23.

40. See Rita L. Moroney, "Postal Reorganization: An Outline," typewritten, files of the postmasters general, U.S. Postal Service, Washington.

41. Dolenga, "Postal Reform," p. 530.

42. There had been an apparent break in the impasse when James Rademacher, president of the National Association of Letter Carriers, and President Richard Nixon met at the White House and reached an agreement that called for union support of a non-corporate "postal authority" in return for White House support for postal pay raises. But the other postal unions and some members of Congress felt displeased over having been excluded from the meeting at which the decision was reached, and the compromise collapsed. (See Dolenga, "Postal Reform," pp. 529–540.)

43. *New York Times*, March 18, 1970, p. 1. The *New York Times* provided exceptionally good coverage throughout the strike, and so did the *Wall Street Journal*.

44. *New York Times*, March 25, 1970, p. 1. Also see Dolenga, "Postal Reform," pp. 540–545.

45. *New York Times*, April 3, 1970, pp. 1, 19. Also see Dolenga, "Postal Reform," pp. 545–550.

46. U.S., Congress, House, *Message from the President of the United States Relative to Postal Reform*, House Document 91–313, 91st Cong., 2d Sess., 1970, p. v.

47. Postmaster General Winton Blount, quoted in Dolenga, "Postal Reform," p. 556.

48. On this point, see Joseph A. Califano, *A Presidential Nation* (New York: W. W. Norton, 1975), pp. 25–30. Califano notes: "Passage of reorganization measures

through the Congress requires a significant investment of political capital by the president himself, and even then significant reform is likely to elude his grasp" (p. 30).

49. For interesting examples of interagency conflicts over reorganization proposals, see *New York Times*, January 23, 1978, pp. 1, 13.

50. Rufus E. Miles, Jr., suggests that efforts to elevate the organizational status of an agency through reorganization may elicit opposition to the measure from other agencies and interests. Miles, "Considerations for a President Bent on Reorganization," *Public Administration Review*, 37 (March/April, 1977), p. 156.

51. For a discussion of the problems experienced by reorganizers when their plans would affect state and local agencies, see Harold Seidman, *Politics, Position, and Power*, 2d ed. (New York: Oxford University Press, 1975), pp. 177–180. And for discussions of the problems of implementing federal programs through state or local agencies, see Jeffrey L. Pressman and Aaron B. Wildavsky, *Implementation* (Berkeley: University of California Press, 1973); and Jerome T. Murphy, "The Educational Bureaucracies Implement Novel Policy: The Politics of Title I of ESEA, 1965–1972," in *Policy and Politics in America: Six Case Studies*, ed. Allan P. Sindler (Boston: Little, Brown, 1973).

Chapter 2

ENHANCING MANAGERIAL CAPACITIES

Once the reorganization's passage was assured, postal executives turned their attention to internal problems of managerial control. While the external image of the postal system was being altered by new graphics and a bold new organizational logo, steps were being taken inside the postal bureaucracy to rid the system of some obvious impediments to businesslike management—obstacles that restricted managerial flexibility, stifled innovation, and discouraged cost-consciousness. Conspicuous among these was a problem involving the organization's front-line managers (the postmasters); they were political patronage appointees whose managerial talents were not always apparent and whose loyalties to the organization often came second to their loyalties to their political patrons. Other problems stemmed from the rigid rules and regulations by which postal headquarters traditionally had tried to guide the system's far-flung operations; these controls stifled managerial initiative and provided local officials with little discretion to adapt organizational policies to the exigencies of local conditions. Finally, postal headquarters lacked an effective and reliable way of assessing the performance of local offices.

Thus, as the Post Office Department underwent its metamorphosis, postal executives initiated efforts to improve internal management. These steps included development of a new merit system for selecting postmasters, alteration of internal management structures and methods to shift greater operating authority to the field, and introduction of new management information systems and perform-

ance measures. Some of these steps were more easily undertaken
and more likely to succeed than others.

Problems in Administrative Management

From the earliest days of the U.S. postal system, one of the primary
tasks facing its top managers has been to find suitable administrative arrangements to counterbalance the system's natural tenden-
cies toward decentralization and fragmentation.[1] Because the
postal system is a complex communications and distribution network, it must be coordinated and controlled from headquarters.
That is, postal facilities, transportation routes, distribution schemes,
and the like all must be arranged and concerted by persons with a
large enough comprehension of the entire network to ensure that a
letter dropped in a collection box on Fifth Avenue in New York
actually has some chance of being delivered to a house on Fifth
Street in Eugene, Oregon, in only a few days. The top-down control
needed for this degree of coordination in operations is also clearly
necessary for maintaining standard personnel practices throughout
the system, for properly accounting for daily postage receipts, for
controlling acquisition of equipment, for preserving the privacy of
the mails, and the like.

But this need for coordination and centralized managerial control has long conflicted with strong pressures, also inherent in the
system, toward decentralization and fragmentation. Perhaps the
most obvious of these decentralizing forces is the sheer size and ge-
ographical distribution of the postal network. With post offices at
over 30,000 sites around the country, the variations in local service
requirements are great, and it is difficult, to say the least, for a centralized administration to develop sensible rules and regulations
that are appropriate everywhere.

For years, another prominent source of fragmentation in postal
management was the political patronage system for selecting postmasters, the organization's most important frontline managers. The
key to postmaster selection was a "political advisor system," which
was neither sanctioned nor recognized in law but which governed
the process nevertheless. Under the political advisor system, a senator, a congressman, or occasionally a local party chairman from the
President's political party was the advisor for each postal district in

the country and effectively reserved the right to choose the local postmaster if a vacancy arose.[2]

Although the Civil Service Commission routinely held competitive examinations for postmaster positions and submitted the top three names to the postmaster general for a choice, the new postmaster actually was not chosen by the postmaster general; the appropriate political advisor made the decision. Conducting examinations and drawing up a civil service register was important only for its obstructive or dilatory capacity, for if the desired candidate was not among the top three qualifiers on the exam, the advisor could refuse to name anyone, preferring instead to wait until a favored candidate finally scored high enough to make the top three. Thus, some post offices went for years without a postmaster, while the examinations were given over and over until the right candidate appeared.[3] Once the Senate confirmed a new postmaster, this person, regardless of actual qualification, automatically achieved full civil service status, receiving all the fringe benefits, retirement protections, and job securities.

The obvious problem with this arrangement, at least from the perspective of headquarters postal officials, was that many postmasters naturally felt more allegiance to their outside political patrons than to their nominal superiors in the department. The political nature of the appointment made the local postmaster quite autonomous, if he chose to be. If a postmaster held enough political power (and many did), he could decide when, if at all, he would let his actions be guided by regional or headquarters "superiors."[4]

But over the years, the old Post Office Department had worked hard to counterbalance these decentralizing forces, trying to ensure the coordination of operations through a rigid hierarchical structure and a steady flow of rules and directives, reinforced by inspections. The department was organized into six bureaus (Operations, Finance and Administration, Personnel, Transportation and International Services, Facilities, and Research and Engineering), plus the Postal Inspection Service and the Office of the General Counsel. This functional organization at headquarters was reflected in the structure of the fifteen regional offices and in the larger post offices also. The headquarters staffs coordinated regional and local operations through a continuous stream of regulations and instructions contained in the *Postal Bulletin* and in constant updates to the enormous *Postal Manual*, the department's nine-pound administrative

bible that contained postal regulations, details on rates, and prescriptions for conduct in the face of almost every imaginable contingency.[5]

The wide span of control in the department's flat hierarchical
structure placed extraordinary emphasis on the manual, making
it an indispensable one-way communication channel between regional directors and local postmasters. Each of the fifteen regional
directors, nominally responsible for all offices within the region, had
an average of 2,200 postmasters reporting to him. Short on staff,
and limited in his own delegated authority, the regional director
could hardly devote much attention to more than a few key offices
and thus had to rely on the manual and supplemental instructions
to communicate with individual offices and to ensure the coordination of activities within the region and among regions.[6]

Adherence to the elaborate code of approved operating procedures was enforced by the Postal Inspection Service, the
department's vigorous internal police force, which conducted surprise inspections of post offices about once a year. Ostensibly acting
to see that postal employees were not embezzling funds, postal inspectors also conducted detailed reviews of local operations and reported irregularities and deviations from *Postal Manual* policies to
the regional directors. In addition, postal inspectors made unan-
nounced visits to inspection galleries, enclosed catwalks suspended
from the ceiling of every post office with more than thirty employees. (The galleries provide one-way views of the floor below and
have entrances at the buildings' exteriors; even the postmaster
sometimes is not aware of being under surveillance.) Thus, adherence to the postal system's codified operating procedures was maintained by the knowledge that deviation could easily be detected.[7]

To the postal reformers of the late 1960s, these means of administrative control appeared deficient in at least two ways. First, managerial creativity and initiative at the local level went unrewarded,
and was even punished, in this system. For field managers, the only
safe course was to follow the book. The result, not surprisingly, was
a very rigid, authoritarian system, well suited to coordination and
to the maintenance of standard operating procedures but resistant
to change, local managerial initiative, and effective cost control.[8]
Managing for economy was impossible at the local level because no
information existed on the costs of operating individual post offices,
and there was no incentive to reduce costs. A postmaster's

"budget" was set in man-hours, not dollars. The postmaster received a specific allocation of man-hours from regional headquarters, and if that allocation was not enough, the postmaster merely asked for additional man-hours—a request routinely granted. Moreover, since a postmaster's salary was set according to how many employees were in his facility, it was in his interest to increase the man-hours as much as possible.[9] Similarly perverse incentives were plentiful in the postal system before 1971.

A second problem troubling postal reformers was the functional organization of the department, which in their view gave too much power to the Bureau of Operations. As the subunit responsible for all mail processing and delivery, Operations accounted for 80 percent of the entire postal budget; more important, it enjoyed virtual veto power over the programs and decisions of the other bureaus, exercising that veto whenever a proposed policy threatened to hinder the quick movement of the mails.[10] In the view of the business-minded postal reformers, the organizational prominence Operations enjoyed (and the resulting preoccupation throughout the organization with day-to-day problems of handling mail) led to insufficient emphasis on controlling costs and insufficient attention to long-range planning and cultivating new markets. Following the reorganization, the reconstituted Postal Service took important steps to alter these long-standing organizational arrangements, to eliminate faulty administrative methods, and to improve internal management. Some of these changes were begun even before the reorganization was formally under way.

Merit Selection of Postmasters

To the proponents of postal reform, the political appointment of postmasters seemed at best an anachronism and at worst a serious obstacle to effective management. Anyhow, it was a problem to be solved as soon as possible. Postal reformers were not alone in holding that view. Good-government forces such as the National Civil Service League also wanted changes; they held the political-advisor system to be inconsistent with the whole concept of merit in government employment and alleged it to have a depressive effect on the morale and aspirations of able and experienced career employees, who could not aspire to the top of the hierarchy in the local office because this post was reserved for political reward.[11] Also, many members of Congress were anxious to see changes on this front since the patronage system carried political liabilities as well as advantages. Former U.S. Senator Thruston B. Morton (Rep., Ky.) expressed the feelings of many of his colleagues when he told a House committee in 1969:[12]

At first glance, this system might appear to be a political plum to a Senator or Representative who is on the advisor list. Actually, the opposite is true. It was one of the biggest pains in the neck I had during my years on the Hill. Every time I recommended the appointment of a postmaster or rural carrier, I lost 50 votes from the others who were not recommended. It was one of those cases where you could not even get to first base, never mind across homeplate. It was damned if you did and damned if you did not.

Thus there was little opposition when, on February 5, 1969, President Richard Nixon and Postmaster General Winton Blount, signaling their commitment to postal reform, announced the abolition by executive order of the political advisor system for appointing postmasters and rural letter carriers. Future appointments, the President declared, would be made "on a merit basis without the usual political clearance." [13] A new element of professionalism was to be introduced into the operation of the postal system; performance, not patronage, would be the byword of the organization. But the Administration's proposal to use "open, competitive civil service exams" to fill all vacancies raised immediate complaints from the postal unions and from congressmen that such a method would diminish promotion opportunities for career employees.

So, two weeks later, on February 19, 1969, Postmaster General Blount announced the details of a selection procedure that took account of these criticisms. The core of the new system was the creation of Management Selection Boards (MSBs) on both national and regional levels. Both the national board, which was to choose postmasters for the 400 largest post offices in the country, and the 15 regional boards, which were to select postmasters for all other (31,800) offices, were to contain at least one postal official familiar with the abilities of staff members at the office involved, and also an official appointed by the Civil Sevice Commission, a person selected by the American Arbitration Association, and at least one person with special competence in management and business administration. Reform-minded postal officials considered this mix of private and public board members the best guarantee of an equitable and authentic merit system. Only if a board could not select a suitable postmaster from the list of three career employees submitted by postal management would a competitive civil service exam be held (open to all postal employees) to choose a new slate of candidates for the board to consider. The new criteria for postmasters were to stress "labor relations capability, race relations sensitivity, experience as a decision-maker, and experience operating within substantial budgets." [14]

The new selection system did not begin operating until August 1970 (when the Postal Reorganization Act was passed and signed into law), although the Post Office Department had been readying the machinery of the new process meanwhile. Thus, on November 29, 1970, eighty-five new postmasters, the first group to be appointed on merit alone, took office. By the end of fiscal 1979, over 23,000 postmasters had been appointed under this merit selection system. [15] This record is important not only because merit appointments may enlist "better" managers (there is, of course, no guarantee of that) but because the new emphasis on appointing postmasters from within the organization has enhanced the upward mobility of postal employees. The architects of the postal reform movement were fond of reciting statistics showing that most postal employees were stuck in the same jobs for most of their careers. The inauguration of the merit system at least improved the chances that craft employees and those in the supervisory ranks might be able to move up in the organization.

The new process for selecting a postmaster was the first significant step toward reconstituting the internal management of the postal system. Other changes were still to come.

Reorganizing Headquarters and Field Management

In the months following passage of the reorganization act, the business executives who held the top positions in the new Postal Service devoted much of their attention to devising a new structure for administrative management. With the dual intention of reorienting top management and delegating more operating authority to the

regional and local offices, Postmaster General Winton Blount initiated a series of massive internal reorganizations, reshaping structures and practices for both headquarters and field management.

In initiating a new headquarters organization in 1971, Blount announced that part of his intention was to "create an organization
that focuses on the major businesses of the Postal Service," and to
make top management more aware of changing customer needs.[16]
Blount already had changed the name of the main subdivisions in
the Postal Service from *bureaus* to *departments.* Similarly, *top staff*
was changed to *top management.* The changes in terminology were
meant to be symbolic of changes in attitude the postmaster general
was trying to instill during the transition year. Blount wanted
postal executives and managers to think of themselves as managers
of a business enterprise, not as administrators of a government department.

But on July 1, 1971 (the day the Post Office Department became
the U.S. Postal Service), Blount went beyond symbolic action, dras-
tically reorganizing his top management team so that the old
procedures of an administrative bureaucracy could be more easily
replaced with businesslike approaches to management.[17] The postmaster general was to be the chief execuive officer, and the position
of deputy postmaster general was strengthened with the intent that
its incumbent would be the chief operating officer. The former bureau (department) structure was abolished. In its place, three senior
assistant postmasters general (to be the equivalent of senior vice
presidents in private business corporations) were designated to head
new management groups. The internal reorganization splintered
the chief responsibilities of the powerful Operations Bureau (mail
processing and delivery), and divided them between two of the new
groups. The first, the Mail Processing Group, was organized to focus new attention on the differences in processing methods required
of the postal system's two main "product lines"—letter mail and
bulk mail. The second group, Customer Services, was established to
develop marketing information (a management task the old Post
Office Department largely ignored) and focus on the organization's
consumer contact activities, including delivery services.

But the attempt to end the Operations Bureau's control over the
disposition of organizational resources faced obstacles; the most
conspicuous was opposition to the change from within Operations
that saw processing mail and delivering it as a coherent set of tasks
rightly belonging within the assured jurisdiction of a single organi-

zational subunit. And in an organization for which moving the mail is both the central task and the organizational ethos, the subunit historically responsible for that movement is bound to have high status and a highly resistant claim to control over organizational resources. Not surprisingly, Blount's successor as postmaster general performed another substantial reshuffling in 1973, reuniting mail processing and delivery services in a new Operations Group, headed by a senior assistant postmaster general (SAPMG), and placing the regional postmasters general in a direct reporting relation to the SAPMG for Operations.[18]

The other, more important internal reorganization initiated by Postmaster General Blount in 1971 was supposed to decentralize operating responsibilities in the postal system by reorganizing administrative arrangements in the field and freeing local managers from the constraints of the rule book. This reorganization created a whole new field structure and established a new approach to postal management. Before these changes, most of the important operating decisions were made by Congress and dictated from headquarters, including some personnel selection, facilities planning, and day-to-day operating practices. Under the new structure, the number of regions was cut from fifteen to five, and the newly designated regional postmasters general were given full responsibility for all postal operations within their regions. All authority not specifically reserved to headquarters (which was thenceforth to be just a top-level support organization, primarily handling matters such as rates and labor negotiations) would be exercised by the regional postmasters general.[19]

This internal reorganization also formalized two new levels of management—the district and the sectional center. Sectional center managers report to a district manager who in turn reports to the regional postmaster general. The forty-seven district offices do not have detailed management responsibilities but serve as extensions of the regional offices, seeing that policies are carried out and assisting field managers with service problems.[20]

This new field structure sought primarily to push responsibility for day-to-day operations out of headquarters to the field, where there was a need for greater managerial flexibility. In a letter to postmasters describing the changes, Blount wrote in 1971:[21]

> It [decentralization] will get away from that strait jacket of the past, whereby the postal system was run by the book and the book was

written in Washington. We want to give managers a chance to manage, to innovate and initiate—and even to make mistakes.

Blount's successor as postmaster general, E. T. Klassen, continued the decentralizing trend through his administration. In March of 1973, Klassen declared: "I am determined to decentralize the system to give our local managers the flexibility to make the thousands of individual decisions that must be made in the course of each work day." [22] In line with this philosophy, field managers and postmasters have been delegated hundreds of items of authority previously exercised by headquarters. And although the *Postal Manual* still adorns every manager's desk, its distilled contents leave field managers with far more discretion over the many decisions that they face daily.

To supplement the delegation of operating authority, the Postal Service has sought (through efforts that have brought the organization acclaim) to improve the ability of these field managers to exercise responsibility intelligently. The Service has undertaken a serious effort to provide innovative, extensive training for newly appointed supervisors, managers, and postmasters; this training is carried out at the Postal Service Management Institute in Bethesda, Maryland. The institute provides instruction in specific areas of postal management (mail processing, delivery services, customer services, labor relations, and finance) and in general business management practices (analyzing problems, making decisions, planning, supervision, control, and communication). [23]

In short, in the decade since the Postal Reorganization Act was passed, the Postal Service has taken steps to enhance its internal managerial capacities. It is now identifying talented and promising employees within the organization, promoting them on the basis of merit to supervisory positions and postmasterships, vesting them with increased discretion and authority, and putting them through high-quality training programs to instill in them good managerial judgment.

It is not altogether clear what difference some of these changes have made. Possibly the politically appointed postmasters operated more efficient and responsive post offices in an effort to cast themselves and their political patrons in a more favorable light. Still, there is no doubt that some of the changes instituted by the Postal Service have eliminated managerial handicaps that debilitated the system for decades. For example, whereas before the reorganization a local postmaster neither worked from a budget nor even had information on the costs of his own office's operations, now he does. The local postmaster now is less bound by the rigid dictates of the organization's rules and regulations. He is encouraged to experiment and introduce new methods—in short, to *manage*, finding ways to hold down costs and improve service.

Yet in spite of these improvements, the Postal Service still faces persistent obstacles to effective managerial control of postal operations. For example, unlike most private business firms, the Postal Service has no independent, external measure of performance such as profit in a competitive market. Hence it is difficult for the Postal Service to establish performance measures that are not subject to employee manipulation. The two cases that follow illustrate the Postal Service's problems in devising reliable performance and productivity measures.

Measuring Delivery Performance

The postal system is a delivery organization whose customers value not only speed of delivery but also consistency (that is, being able to predict accurately how long delivery will take between two points). Yet for years the old Post Office Department had no formal goals for delivery performance. It simply delivered the mail as quickly as possible, and that was that. The department did have a relatively primitive system, however, for gathering data for internal use on the actual transmission times for first-class mail. From 1954 to 1967, the Post Office's principal test of delivery time involved periodic test mailings to measure the elapsed time between deposit of test letters in a collection box and actual delivery to a home or an office. The Post Office Department conducted nationwide test mailings several times each year, using about 350,000 pieces of air mail and first-class and special delivery letters, and involving the 175 largest post offices in the country. The tests mainly consisted of the interchange of letters between individuals living in 150 test cities. When postal headquarters finished compiling the results of the periodic tests, it rated the regions and post offices according to performance. Headquarters analysts based these ratings on a comparison of the test results with the time it should have taken each piece of mail to move through the system, according to the actual pickup, processing, transportation, and delivery schemes and schedules.[24]

But the performance ratings were not taken seriously and the test results were not used earnestly for managerial purposes, partly because fundamental weaknesses in the testing method made the results less than satisfactory indicators of actual performance. For example, the system used special test envelopes, easily identifiable by postal employees, who could give them expedited treatment. The studies also used postal employees, not outsiders, as the recipients of test letters, further increasing the possibility of manipulating data. Finally, the tests compared actual transmission times with somewhat unrealistic "scheduled" times.[25]

Thus, when the new Postal Service established formal delivery standards, it also needed a more sophisticated information system that could collect, analyze, and present mail delivery data. The delivery standards, first announced in 1971, are one-day (overnight) delivery within local areas, two-day delivery within a 600-mile radius, and three-day delivery to all other areas. These standards apply only to first-class mail that has proper address and Zip Code and is posted by the designated collection time, generally 5:00 P.M. The Postal Service goal is to meet these standards 95 per cent of the time.

The new information system, called the Origin-Destination Information System (ODIS), uses sampling techniques to measure how well the Postal Service is doing in meeting its delivery standards. Although ODIS is a far more advanced testing system than its predecessors, it has some conspicuous deficiencies. Unlike the old nationwide test, ODIS measures the interval not from time of posting to time of delivery but from the time a letter is *postmarked* to the time it is received in the last postal facility before being delivered to the addressee. Thus, actual transmission time for a letter may be as much as a couple of days longer than the figures suggest, depending on how long it sits in a collection box before being picked up, how long it sits in a post office before being postmarked, and how long it takes the carrier to deliver it.[26]

A more important deficiency of the ODIS measure stems partly from the double use to which the system's data are put. When headquarters managers developed the new measuring system, they wanted to generate data that would be used both in controlling the quality of delivery service *and* in judging performance throughout the system. Thus, raw ODIS data are gathered from all over the country, and the results are distributed to the regions, districts, and individual post offices. Postal officials at each level use the results to judge the performance of the next-lower level; headquarters judges the regions, the regions judge district performances, and so on, down to the individual facilities.

This use of ODIS data as a performance measure soon led to fairly widespread manipulation of the system by anxious local postal officials. Investigations by General Accounting Office (GAO) auditors and postal inspectors in the mid-1970s revealed that some local postal managers were manipulating the ODIS system and its scores. In Detroit, GAO investigators found, late mail was deliberately being removed from delivery units before ODIS tests to improve overnight delivery statistics. Three Detroit mail-processing foremen told the investigators that they had been instructed to examine mail scheduled for ODIS testing and to remove letters that already were late according to Postal Service delivery standards. They then reinserted these letters in the mail-processing operation at a point when the letters could not reach the delivery unit in time to be included in the ODIS test.[27]

Other, less overt methods of manipulating ODIS data also appear to have been fairly common practice at times. Since notice of ODIS test dates and of units to be tested is given to mail-processing officials at most sectional center facilities (SCFs) well in advance, these managers have an opportunity to expedite mail destined to delivery units scheduled for testing. At the Houston SCF, for example, mail-processing and quality-control officials admitted to increasing staff power at units to be tested in order to avoid possible repercussions from higher management about low test scores.[28]

The Postal Service experienced similar problems with another information system it introduced to help local managers use their available manpower more productively in meeting work loads.

Systems for Reporting the Work Load

Executives in the new Postal Service recognized that even if the organization were successful at recruiting able field managers on the basis of merit, and at training them and vesting them with more operating authority, the real test of managerial competence would be whether the organization's resources were being used productively.

In the postal system, the chief resources are labor, capital and the mail itself. The management problem in the Postal Service is to use these resources in the best productive mixture for producing the organization's output, namely, the processed and delivered mail. But reaching a favorable productive mixture is complicated in that senders post mail primarily at their own convenience, not that of the post office. This results in tremendous fluctuations in work load throughout the day in large post offices across the country. Local managers face the difficult problem of making sure they have enough workers on hand to process the peak loads without having more than are necessary. They must also keep all the people who are needed to process mail during heavy periods productively occupied during slack periods.

In years past, postal officials relied on third-class mail (much of it advertising circulars, popularly known as junk mail) to help smooth out the work load. Since post offices are not committed to moving this mail as quickly as first-class items, third-class typically has been held off for processing during "slow" hours. However, the postal system's various efforts over the years to achieve greater efficiency in processing mail have reduced the effectiveness of third-class mail as a device for maintaining a more uniform total work load. The Postal Service's encouragement, for example, of presorting bulk mail (mailers are offered discounted postage rates if they presort their items by Zip Code) has decreased the amount of processing that bulk-rate third-class mail needs, thus reducing its effectiveness as a flywheel.[29]

Since the productivity of the Postal Service depends in no small measure on the extent to which local managers are effective in making their manpower scheduling decisions, postal headquarters has sought to institute management-control systems to aid local managers in this process.

The Postal Service, relying on the advice of McKinsey and Company, management consultants, instituted a computerized data system, the Work Load Reporting System (WLRS), to calculate mail volume, work hours, and cost relations for 70 different mail-processing operations. For each post office tied into the system (generally limited to the nation's largest post offices), the WLRS computer produced detailed output reports by shift, day, week, and accounting period. Originally, these data were intended to help local managers in scheduling manpower to meet expected mail volumes, and to help management at all levels in evaluating the effects of technological improvements and changes in methods of processing mail.[30]

But to top management, the WLRS seemed to provide an irresistible additional opportunity—the chance to apply the data on a national basis to evaluate performance of line supervisors, individual post offices, and entire regions, and to compare or rank post offices and regions according to productivity performance. Accordingly, with data furnished by WLRS, headquarters officials instituted the *Eighty Office Productivity Index Report*, which ranked, from best to worst, the performance of the eighty largest post offices.[31] In short, officials at headquarters were trying to use the new WLRS data to stimulate internal competition in the postal system and to provide local managers with an incentive to use labor as efficiently as possible in meeting their work loads.

Within two years it became clear that this application of the WLRS data had undermined the original purpose of the system, which was to help local managers in making immediate decisions about staffing to meet the fluctuations in work load efficiently. Pressures on the managers and employees of the largest post offices to excel in the intensifying interoffice competition led to widespread falsification of WLRS data. Since it was extraordinarily difficult for an office to achieve real productivity increases, and since cutting personnel would affect office showings on other performance ratings (such as ODIS), a local manager who wanted to show a strong improvement in the productivity rankings could do so more easily by *appearing* to process more mail with the same (or even a smaller) number of employees.

Thus by early 1973, headquarters officials were finding that falsifying WLRS data was widespread in the field. One common method of adulteration involved the treatment of presorted or "riffle" mail (items presorted by the customer in Zip Code sequence). A simple riffling procedure (that is, quickly sliding the thumb along the edge of the envelopes) is enough to sort this mail quickly. Some local managers inflated their office productivity measures (some by as much as 25 times) by improperly crediting this presorted mail to manual sorting operations, thereby indicating greater productivity than what really existed.[32]

Another, more serious and more widespread falsification was made possible by the shift under WLRS from linear measurement of mail volume to weight measurement on automated electronic scales that transmitted volume data directly to Postal Service computers. Internal audits throughout the postal system in 1974 revealed repeated cases of deliberate inflation of volume figures; managers would have employees run the same mail over the mechanized weight-recording system up to eight times before sending it on to the next processing step. Postal inspectors discovered serious volume inflations by this practice in San Francisco, Washington, Philadelphia, Houston, and many other cities.[33]

The Washington Post Office, for example, experienced a remarkable rise in the reported productivity of its mail-processing operations. In just a couple of years, Washington had moved from a relatively low standing among the 80 largest offices to near the number one position on the *Eighty Office Productivity Index Report*. The improved relative standing was the result of reported (though false) increases in mail volume handled without a corresponding increase in man-hours used. A 1974 investigation of the Washington office revealed that total piece handlings there may have been inflated by more than 110 per cent. The officials responsible for these distortions of WLRS data generally attributed their conduct to excessive pressure from higher management to achieve unrealistic productivity goals and to the belief that failure to do so would hurt their careers.[34]

In short, this effort by top officials to extend the use of the WLRS data hampered the information system's effectiveness as an everyday managerial tool for efficient manpower scheduling. As one top postal official said, in trying to explain the problem to a congressional investigating committee in 1976: "In brief, the system tended to nurture the managing of numbers or 'productivity statistics' rather than of people and of actual work volumes." [35] This is a form of "goal displacement," familiar to students of bureaucratic organizations. An instrument such as the statistical index, intended to further the accomplishment of organizational objectives, becomes an end in itself. Employees begin to think of maximizing the indexes as their main goal, sometimes at the expense of the original objective.[36]

As a result of the distortions in the data produced by WLRS, postal officials were forced to abandon the system. They replaced it in 1975 with a simplified system of recording work loads (the Management Operating Data System), the sole purpose of which has been to help local managers in evaluating changes in work loads and man-hours so they can plan budgets. In 1980 the Postal Service prepared to install yet another new system—the National Workhour Reporting System—in the hope of producing more refined data for planning, budgeting, and reporting work hours. The continual development of new information systems reflects an increased emphasis inside the Postal Service on producing useful data for managerial purposes; and it can also be seen as part of a continuing process of "organizational learning," whereby the organization adapts as a result of experience. Both are salutary trends, likely to produce better management systems over time.[37]

But the Postal Service still has no adequate productivity measure, no meaningful way of comparing management techniques of different post offices or for comparing the whole organization with other enterprises. The reason is that the Postal Service has no independent, external standard, such as profit in a competitive market, against which to measure organizational performance. If it had, it could go beyond its simple and inadequate ratio of total man-years to mail volume and judge individual offices (and the organization as a whole) with measures such as profits per man-hour and profits per dollar of wages. Since no independent, external standard exists, it is understandable that the Postal Service finds it difficult to devise even partly worthwhile measures that are not subject to manipulation.

Since the Postal Service has decided that its best approximation of a useful performance measure is the ratio of total man-years to total mail volume, the organization devotes much of its efforts to increasing the efficiency of postal operations—that is, devising methods to enable the existing number of employees to process more mail in the same period, or instituting practices that will reduce the number of persons needed to process a given amount of mail.

It is logical next to examine some of the obstacles postal management has faced in trying to work out methods of controlling labor costs and improving the efficiency of postal operations. Readers conversant with governmental operations will not be surprised that these cost-cutting efforts have run aground whenever they have led to reductions in services the public has come to expect or when they have violated the interests of politically powerful groups, inside or outside the Postal Service.

Endnotes

1. For a fascinating account of the bold administrative efforts by Amos Kendall (President Andrew Jackson's postmaster general) to centralize control over postal operations, see Matthew A. Crenson, *The Federal Machine: Beginnings of Bureaucracy in Jacksonian America* (Baltimore: The Johns Hopkins University Press, 1975).
2. "New Era Favors Career Postmasters," *Postal Life* (May 1969), pp. 8–11.
3. *Ibid.*
4. President's Commission on Postal Organization, Report of the Commission, *Towards Postal Excellence* (Washington: U.S. Government Printing Office, 1968), Annex, vol. 3, part 4, p. 25.
5. *Ibid.*, part 3, p. 66.
6. *Ibid.*, part 2, p. 13.
7. For an illuminating discussion of the methods a bureaucratic organization can use to detect and discourage deviation from standard procedures, see Herbert Kaufman, *The Forest Ranger: A Study in Administrative Behavior* (Baltimore: The Johns Hopkins University Press, 1960), chaps. 4 and 5.
8. President's Commission on Postal Organization, *Towards Postal Excellence*, Annex, vol. 3, part 3, p. 66.
9. President's Commission on Postal Organization, *Towards Postal Excellence*, p. 28.
10. President's Commission on Postal Organization, Annex, vol. 1, part 1, p. 44; vol. 3, part 2, p. 13. For more on the prominence of the Operations Bureau, see Donald F. Bogue, "Resource Allocation in the Postal System of the United States from an Opportunity Set Perspective." (Senior honors thesis, Harvard University, 1973), pp. 39–43.
11. "New Era Favors Career Postmasters," *Postal Life* (May 1969), p. 11.
12. U.S. Congress, House, Committee on Post Office and Civil Service, *Post Office Reorganization, Hearings before the Committee on Post Office and Civil Service*, 91st Cong., 1st Sess., 1969, p. 600.
13. Richard Nixon, quoted in "New Era Favors Career Postmasters," *Postal Life* (May 1969), p. 11.
14. U.S. Post Office Department, Information Service, General Release No. 39, February 19, 1969.
15. U.S. Postal Service, *Comprehensive Statement on Postal Operations* (January 1980), p. 3.
16. U.S. Postal Service, General Release No. 48, May 12, 1971.
17. The internal reorganization was first announced on May 12, 1971, and effected on July 1, 1971. See U.S. Postal Service, General Release No. 48, May 12, 1971.

18. "Postal Service: Organization and Administration—Modification of Organization and Reporting Relationships," *Federal Register,* 38, no. 146, July 31, 1973, pp. 20402–20415; or see "Headquarters Staff Restructured," *Postal Leader,* July 1973, p. 1.
19. "Reorganization Seeks to Strengthen Field," *Postal Leader,* June 1971, pp. 1, 4.
20. *Ibid.*
21. Winton M. Blount to postmasters, June 1, 1971, in files of the Postmaster General, U.S. Postal Service, Washington.
22. Quoted in *Union Postal Clerk,* April 1, 1973, p. 3.
23. For more on the Postal Service Management Institute, see Robert J. Myers, *The Coming Collapse of the Post Office* (Englewood Cliffs, N.J.: Prentice-Hall, 1975), pp. 85–89. The institute is one of the few features of the Postal Service that Myers (publisher of the *New Republic*) singles out for praise in an otherwise highly censorious look at the postal system.
24. President's Commission on Postal Organization, *Towards Postal Excellence,* Annex, vol. 3, part 4, pp. 83–84.
25. *Ibid.,* part 2, pp. 43–47.
26. Comptroller General of the United States, *System for Measuring Mail Delivery Performance—Its Accuracy and Limits,* report to the Congress (Washington: General Accounting Office, October 17, 1975), p. 2.
27. *Ibid.,* pp. 8–17.
28. *Ibid.,* p. 11.
29. President's Commission on Postal Organization, *Towards Postal Excellence,* Annex, vol. 3, part 4, p. 69.
30. U.S. Congress, House, Committee on Post Office and Civil Service, *Operation of the Washington, D.C., Post Office, Hearings before a subcommittee of the Committee on Post Office and Civil Service,* 94th Cong., 2d Sess., 1976, pp. 2–8.
31. *Ibid.,* p. 4.
32. *Ibid.*
33. *Ibid.,* pp. 4–6.
34. *Ibid.*
35. *Ibid.,* p. 7.
36. "Displacement of goals" is a concept developed in Robert K. Merton, *Social Theory and Social Structure,* rev. ed. (Glencoe, Ill.: Free Press, 1957), pp. 199, 200. Examples abound in the literature. See, for example, Peter M. Blau, *The Dynamics of Bureaucracy,* rev. ed. (Chicago: Univ. of Chicago Press, 1963), pp. 45–46, 232–233, and 239–241.
37. On "organizational learning," see Richard Cyert and James March, *A Behavioral Theory of the Firm* (Englewood Cliffs, N.J.: Prentice-Hall, 1963), pp. 123–125.

Chapter 3

OBSTACLES IN CONTROLLING COSTS

The advocates of postal reorganization saw the movement as an opportunity to "take politics out of the postal system" and make postal management more businesslike. "Businesslike" management meant, to those who wanted to see it in the postal system, management that would apply modern technical and managerial knowhow to the system's anachronistic operations, and implement new efficiency schemes and productivity improvement programs; it meant, in short, management that above all would stress increasing productivity and controlling costs.

In the labor-intensive Postal Service, controlling costs is synonymous with controlling *labor* costs, since employee wages and benefits account for 86 percent of the system's total costs.[1] Thus, the most direct cost-control method would involve holding back the rate of increase in employee wages and benefits. But successful pursuit of that strategy is difficult at best. Some of the main alternative cost-control methods the Postal Service has pursued are a job freeze, new technological procedures, altered work methods, and new programs to increase operating efficiency. Taking such steps is seldom easy, even under the best circumstances. But postal management's efforts to apply many of these cost-cutting methods have also been sharply circumscribed by other factors. They include the formidable legacy of inefficient operations inherited from the Post Office Department and, more important, the persistent external political demands and strong opposition from postal employees.

A Legacy of Outmoded Operations

The postal system, at the time of its reorganization, faced some
challenges in the efficient performance of basic operations. First,
the postal system was struggling with a tremendous expansion in its
work load. In the period of great national economic growth between 1945 and the start of the postal reform movement in 1967,
the annual torrent of mail pouring into the postal system swelled
from 38 billion pieces to 78 billion.[2] At the same time, extraordinary growth in the number of delivery points overburdened the
system's delivery force. With the rapid construction of new residential and office buildings, and especially with the acceleration of suburban sprawl, the number of daily delivery stops increased in that
period by 1.5 to 2 million a year.[3]

A second operating problem in the years before the reorganization stemmed from the revolutionary changes the nation had witnessed in its transportation modes and patterns. For decades, most
of the nation's mail had moved by train.[4] This was a reliable and
speedy means of moving mail, since in railway mail cars the mail
could be sorted en route. The whole physical plant of the postal
system had been built around this dependence on trains. Seventy-
five of the nation's largest post offices, which handled over 50 per
cent of all mail, stood in central cities near railroad terminals. But
in the 1950s, the nation's transportation system began to undergo
tremendous changes. Trucks and airplanes began to replace trains
as the principal means of transport. Thus, by the mid-1960s, with
only 900 trains in daily general use (down from 10,000 a decade
earlier), movement of mail depended primarily on trucks that had
to go through traffic-choked cities to reach the big postal facilities;
there they often had to line up for hours, awaiting access to inadequate loading docks built long before the huge tractor-trailer was
designed.[5]

Third, in spite of the expansion in work load and the technological changes going on, the Post Office suffered from retarded industrial development. While other industries continually engaged in
research and development to cut costs and improve operations, the

Post Office did not even have a research program of its own until after World War II. Even then, inadequate congressional appropriations and the low importance of the program stunted the development of new machinery, equipment, and physical plants.[6] This underdevelopment was most apparent inside post offices, where mail-handling methods remained much the same as they had been a century earlier. Clerks still stood before the familiar pigeonhole cases, sorting letters by hand at the rate of about thirty a minute. Antiquated facilities hindered mechanization; weak floors would not support heavy machinery, low ceilings ruled out overhead conveyor systems, and vertical building layouts defied any attempt at instituting more efficient horizontal mail-flow systems.[7]

In short, by the late 1960s, the postal system found itself squeezed by the inadequacies of its own industrial development and by circumstances beyond its control. Volume was rising, the population was shifting to new centers outside the central cities, and long-established transportation patterns were changing. The collective stress of these developments presented the Post Office with soaring costs and left it with little choice in handling the mail except to hire more employees. "The idea," one postal official conceded in 1959, "is that if you have a mass of bodies, you can *smother* the mail, and get it delivered by sheer weight of numbers."[8] Such was the philosophy underlying the mushrooming of the department's payroll by 1970 to an all-time high of 741,216 persons. And such was the legacy received by officials of the new Postal Service as they set out to control costs and increase the efficiency of postal operations.

The Postal Service adopted varied programs and policies toward these ends. Unfortunately, the necessity of presenting these efforts here sequentially makes it seem as if postal management has moved confusedly from one strategy to another, trying new approaches as it found its way repeatedly blocked. This has not been the case; these efforts should be understood as constituting a comprehensive managerial approach to controlling cost and improving productivity. Although the Postal Service could not carry out some of the plans, because of effective opposition, these efforts can nevertheless be thought of as further examples of an important organizational learning process that was going on during the 1970s within this newly cost-conscious enterprise.

The Hiring Freeze of 1972

Perhaps the most direct action postal executives took to control costs came late in March 1972, not quite a full year after the reorganization took effect. Although existing labor contracts did not allow him to lay off any workers, Postmaster General E. T. Klassen was intent on trimming labor costs and announced a 90-day freeze on all hiring in the Postal Service. Klassen hoped that the organization's normally high attrition rate would shorten the payroll enough to avert a possible $430 million rate increase.[9]

And only five months after the hiring freeze had been imposed, the Postal Service's financial picture actually seemed to be brightening. Along with the usual attrition of staff and an intensive campaign to encourage early retirements, the hiring freeze had succeeded in reducing the postal work force by 33,000 persons. A happy Klassen announced that the staff cuts and other austerity moves (for example, reduced frequency of collections from street-corner deposit boxes and curtailed Saturday window service in post offices) should enable the Postal Service to avoid the rate increase.[10]

Soon, however, some negative effects of the staff cuts became apparent. Not only were post offices operating with fewer workers but the generous provisions of the early retirement plan had enticed thousands of the more experienced frontline supervisors and postal clerks to leave their jobs. Unfortunately, these departures came during a year when mail volume was increasing by fourteen times the previous year's rate of increase. By the end of the year, the Postal Service quite simply did not have enough experienced employees to handle the massive Christmas mail rush.

In December 1972 and January 1973, the ensuing public outrage over poor postal service spilled onto the editorial pages of newspapers across the country. By February, Postmaster General Klassen was forced to concede publicly that the efforts in controlling costs had resulted in a "serious deterioration" of service throughout the country, with service in some areas (such as the New York metropolitan area) particularly hard hit by the staff reductions.[11]

So much mail condemning the poor quality of postal service flowed into congressional offices that committees in both houses of Congress launched full investigative hearings on the performance of the Postal Service in the 20-month period since the reorganization had taken effect.[12] Citizens complained of extraordinary delays in receiving mail. Postal Service statistics showed that piles of unprocessed mail sat in post offices across the country. Postal union leaders charged that the organization's poor performance resulted from "gross mismanagement" and "blind budget worship." [13] Top postal officials, for their part, admitted that the personnel reductions "may have gone too far." [14] Postmaster General Klassen told a Senate committee: "We may have been so hell-bent on reducing costs that we perhaps lost track of services." [15]

In other words, although the freeze helped reduce the net financial loss for the Postal Service in fiscal 1973 to only $13 million (the lowest it had been since 1945), the reaction of the public and of elected officials to deterioration in service forced postal executives to abandon the direct cost-cutting strategy of reducing staff. Consequently in 1974 postal employment totals shot back up, and the 1974 Postal Service deficit reached $438 million, thirty-three times what it had been in 1973.[16]

Though the option of rapid work force reductions seemed effectively foreclosed, the Postal Service had also been mechanizing its mail processing and delivery methods as part of the effort to control costs and increase productivity. But the mechanization programs also encountered difficulties, and the effects have not been entirely salutary.

New Methods for Processing and Handling Mail

The Post Office employed almost 1 per cent of the whole United States labor force in the late 1960s; this large number of workers was needed partly because the department was still trying to handle 85 billion pieces of mail per year with antiquated processing methods. Not until 1963, when the Zip (Zone Improvement Plan) Code was introduced, was the way opened for fundamental changes in conducting basic postal operations.[17]

Before the Zip Code was initiated, post offices in the United States, in effect, exchanged mail with each of the others. But the Zip Code system divided the United States into ten large geographic areas, assigning to each a number from zero to nine—to become the first digit in a five-digit Zip Code number. Key post offices in each area are designated sectional centers, and each of these is assigned two numbers, which make up the second and third digits in the code. Finally, local post offices within a sectional center's area are designated by the last two digits. (The same system applies to big cities and delivery units within such cities.)[18]

What is important about the Zip Code is that with its advent and with the institution of sectional centers, certain changes became possible in processing and delivering mail. First, with simple, five-digit codes designating specific destinations around the country, clerks could sort by numbers, thereby eliminating much of the memorization of sorting schemes and the like that were previously requisite. This meant also that it was possible to develop machines to expedite sorting. Moreover, a central postal facility—the sectional center—could be designated to process most of the outgoing mail for all post offices in a given area.

By the time the postal reorganization was enacted, the Postal Service was able to make these changes. After a decade of experimentation, new mechanical processing techniques were ready to be used. And partly as a consequence of this new mechanization, the Postal Service was prepared to make fundamental changes in internal mail-routing systems and patterns of predelivery mail movement.

The new mechanical equipment has made fundamental changes in internal postal operations. Though workers continue to handle mail manually in the early processing stages, subsequent steps have the assistance of a wide variety of machinery. For example, processing of outgoing mail (that is, raw mail that needs to be postmarked, sorted, and sent toward its destination) begins when this mail is separated by class, bulk, and dimension. At this culling stage, items of unusual size or shape that must be handled manually are separated from first-class cards and envelopes that generally can be processed on machines. Most machinable mail then goes through a technically sophisticated device called an automatic facer-canceller. At the rate of 20,000 letters an hour, this machine scans the upper right and lower left corners of every envelope, imprinting the cancellation mark if it finds the stamp. If not, the machine instantaneously flips the letter over and scans it a second time. Those with no stamp are rejected; the others are stacked automatically in preparation for the next step, which is sorting by the operators of letter-sorting machines (LSMs).[19]

Each LSM operator sits at a keyboard console where, sixty times a minute, a rotating metal arm reaches into a nearby tray of letters and pushes one onto an automatic conveyor and into the view of the operator, who has six tenths of a second to read the Zip Code before he hears a click. Then, within the next four tenths of a second, the operator must press the three keys corresponding to the first three numbers in the code, causing the letter to be conveyed by electromechanical signal to one of 277 specific destination bins. Simultaneously, the metal arm deposits another letter before the operator.[20]

Each of the destination bins is periodically emptied. Any local mail (that is, mail destined for delivery within the immediate three-digit area) is then further sorted to specific post offices (the last two digits) and to carrier routes (two additional digits used now only by the Postal Service). Mail leaving the area is transported to destination sectional centers, where possibly as soon as the next morning it is sorted by post office and carrier route.

Since cost-effective operation of the expensive new machinery requires substantial mail volume, the Postal Service initiated in 1971 a new program to consolidate mail processing at facilities equipped with letter-sorting machinery. Under this "Area Mail Processing" program, incoming and outgoing mail for local post offices within a designated area is consolidated at a mechanized central processing facility (sometimes referred to as an area mail-processing center; there were 395 of these in 1978) for postmarking, sorting, and dispatch. This presumably allows the Postal Service to reduce costs by making more efficient use of workers, transportation, and mechanized letter-sorting equipment.[21]

The sorting machinery has contributed substantially to improving the postal system's gross productivity figures. The twelve operators of a multiposition letter-sorting machine (MPLSM) can, for example, sort up to 43,200 letters an hour and can sort letters to about five times the number of cities that manual sorting allows; the number of letters that need several sortings is thereby reduced. A fully operational MPLSM can thus handle more mail than forty clerks manually sorting letters before the conventional pigeonhole cases. Largely because of this increased use of sorting machinery, the postal system's gross productivity (the number of pieces of mail processed per postal man-year) increased 23.4 per cent between fiscal 1971 (the last year before postal reorganization) and fiscal 1979. Although the new machinery thus has the clear advantage of permitting fewer persons to process more mail, apparently at a lower cost per unit, it has some conspicuous drawbacks.

A letter sorted by machine is far more likely than a manually sorted letter to be sent astray (and thus delayed) because of a sorting error. And since by 1979 almost three times more letters were being sorted mechanically than in 1969, the absolute number of letters being misdirected and delayed has increased substantially. Because an improperly routed letter requires many additional handlings before it is correctly delivered, these errors are expensive to the Postal Service both in financial costs and public dissatisfaction. With an annual first-class letter volume of 58 billion pieces (in 1979), even a 1 per cent error rate would amount to almost 600 million errors (and irritations) each year. A study the General Accounting Office conducted revealed that the real error rate may be as high as 7 per cent.[22]

Finally, apart from these obviously untoward effects of mechanization, it is also clear that no further productivity improvements are likely to result from it. The Postal Service admits that it is "approaching the saturation point" in its use of the new sorting equipment. "No significant improvement in producivity is expected in the near future from this means."[23] The next big jump in mail-processing productivity is not expected to come until the late 1980s, after installation of new optical character reading and sorting equipment and new bar-code reader-sorters, which will provide for more economical and accurate sorting of mail. These new systems are expected to enhance the effectiveness of another innovation—the expansion of the Zip Code from five to nine digits, which is also expected to increase economies in mail sorting and to speed delivery. The expanded Zip Code will permit unique codes to be given to individual city blocks, to individual apartment buildings and small office buildings, to large buildings by floors or groups of floors, and even to individual firms that have sufficiently large daily mail volumes.[24]

The Bulk-Mail System

Although the Postal Service has been substantially changing its methods of processing letter mail, it has undertaken even more conspicuous alterations in its handling of bulk mail (parcels, books, records, circulars, and some newspapers and magazines not requiring preferential treatment). In years past, bulk mail had always been processed in post offices along with letter mail. But in 1971, arguing that processing both letters and bulk mail in the same facilities was "like trying to manufacture tractors and sports cars on the same assembly line," Postmaster General Winton Blount announced plans to spend $1 billion for construction of a separate network of twenty-one huge facilities for processing bulk mail. Blount said that these facilities ("bulk-mail centers") would use modern sorting equipment designed to reduce handling time and also keep damage to a minimum; they would be located outside congested urban centers but near main transportation lines; and they would cut Postal Service operating costs by at least $300 million and possibly $500 million a year.[25] The Blount management team also hoped the National Bulk Mail System would improve bulk-mail handling enough to stem the flow of parcel-delivery business away from the postal system toward the United Parcel Service and other competitors in the market for shipping small parcels.

All these beneficial effects were expected to flow from the new system (completed in late 1975) because the concentration of bulk mail at these 21 new highly automated facilities would presumably let the Postal Service achieve economies of scale in processing and also lead to more efficient and economical use of transportation; these benefits would derive from the reduction in the number of shipping points from 73 to 21, and the Postal Service could then move greater volumes of mail over fewer routes.[26]

As of this writing, however, few of the expected benefits of the National Bulk Mail System have come to pass. And on some scores things have grown worse. Concerning parcel damage, for example, congressional investigations have revealed that because of faulty building layouts and equipment designs, when the system was first operating millions of packages a year were crushed by the conveyor systems and by the sorting machinery used in the facilities. This problem essentially came about because the Postal Service had continued to use canvas sacks to transport packages, a practice sufficient in itself to weaken many packages. But at the bulk-mail centers, these sacks were emptied by sack-shakeout machines, which turned the sacks upside down and allowed parcels to fall on a flat conveyor covered by impact-absorbing cones. Parcels near the lip of the sacks dropped one foot (the maximum drop according to the design criteria), and those that were at the bottom of the now-inverted sacks could drop as much as four feet. If a parcel got caught in the folds of a sack as it moved away, the package could then drop as much as seven feet to the floor, perhaps smashing apart.

A 1976 report by the Postal Inspection Service noted that this first drop was only the start of a series of shocks a parcel received as it made its way through a bulk-mail center; the report suggested that smashed parcels were most frequently the result of accumulated damage within a center. The report added:[27]

> *If a parcel had only one drop point, only one point at which parcels become crowded, stacked, and changed direction by 90 degrees, almost every parcel would be distributed undamaged; however, such is not the case. After a parcel experiences the shock of unloading from a BMC [bulk mail center] container, that same parcel will be subjected to nine or more drops varying from 12" to 36" or potentially more.*

Thus weakened, many packages were crushed by the sorting equipment or simply torn open when hit by heavier parcels during the sorting. The problem was so serious in 1976 that in the Chicago bulk-mail center alone, more than 3.7 million items (70 per cent of them books) were "loose in the mails." That is, these items had come out of badly damaged packages and become separated from them and thus could neither be delivered nor returned to the sender.[28]

Naturally, the Postal Service eventually modified the equipment to reduce such damage, focusing its attention on redesigning the container unloaders and sack-shakeout machines. These modifications have slowed the speed of parcels as they pour down chutes and conveyors and have also reduced the distance parcels must drop at various places inside the bulk-mail centers.[29] Moreover, the Postal Service installed stations at various equipment locations where employees cull out damaged parcels so that those with only minor damage (torn string and paper, loose tape, and the like) are not further damaged. Also as part of its effort to reduce the amount of damage, the Postal Service (1) has encouraged local post offices not to accept parcels that do not meet the Service's packaging standards; (2) deals directly with large mailers (book publishers and record clubs, and the like) to ensure proper parcel packaging; and (3) manually processes heavy parcels that could damage other packages (book shipments weighing more than 25 pounds, for example, are processed manually).[30]

These improvements and changes sharply reduced within only a couple of years the rate for major damage (that is, damage severe enough to require the parcel to be removed from the mailstream and sent to a separate station to be rewrapped). The rate for major damage fell from 1 per cent (1 package of every 100) in 1975–1976 to 0.26 per cent (2.6 parcels per 1,000) in 1977, and to 0.1 per cent (1 in every 1,000) in fiscal 1978.[31]

Besides the parcel damage problem, a problem existed in the new bulk-mail system with "misdirected mail," or mail sent to the wrong destination. The reasons for this problem are not unlike the problems with sorting letter mail. In the bulk-mail sorting, parcels, once freed from their sacks, slide or tumble down a smooth metal incline toward one of many sorting consoles. There, a sorting clerk working at a keyboard reads the Zip Code and punches the first three numbers onto the keyboard. Those numbers enter a computer that controls a moving tray onto which the package is instantly flipped. If the clerk has punched a code for Chicago (606), the package is ejected from the moving tray just as it passes a down chute exclusively for Chicago. Thus, misdirecting occurs easily when, for example, a parcel addressed to New York is being sorted in Washington, and the clerk punches the wrong sorting keys, mistakenly sending the package to the San Francisco center. These errors obviously result in delivery delays and in increased processing costs, since the mail must be reprocessed and retransported.

In the early years of the bulk-mail system's operation, misdirected mail was a severe problem. In 1975, to cite a particularly serious case, the Chicago center reported misdirected mail rates over a 15-week period ranging from 9.4 per cent to 29.8 per cent of the total mail processed.[32] Through more vigorous training programs for keyboard operators, and better quality-control efforts, the Service has reduced the misdirected rate for bulk mail to roughly 3 percent.[33]

Although the Postal Service has made good progress in reducing the rates of damaged and misdirected bulk mail, it has not been successful in improving the parcel post delivery service, which is inconsistent and slow—slower, in fact, than before the bulk-mail system was built. The General Accounting Office, tracking packages mailed from Washington, D.C., in July and August of 1977, found that only 13 per cent arrived at their destination in Chicago within the four-day delivery period required by the delivery service standards. It was eleven days before 95 per cent of the packages mailed from Washington to San Francisco reached the West Coast.[34]

But slowness is not the worst of the delivery service problems. Market research conducted by the Postal Service indicates that parcel shippers care more about the predictability and consistency of delivery than about the absolute speed. Even so, according to tests reported by the General Accounting Office, the Postal Service's parcel delivery is remarkably inconsistent. For example, delivery standards call for 3.5-day delivery between Chicago and Detroit. When the GAO tested parcel delivery between these two cities over a 10-week period in 1977, it found that only 28 per cent of the parcels met the delivery standards; 45 per cent took 4 to 6 days; 18 per cent took 7 to 10 days; 7 per cent took 11 to 15 days; and 2 per cent took over 15 days.[35]

All these problems taken together (along with the high rates the Postal Service charges for parcel service) have made it difficult for the bulk-mail system to meet its intended goals—stemming the diversion of parcel business away from the Postal Service and helping to control costs. Not only has the Postal Service failed to attract a share of the new growth in the small-parcel-delivery market but its annual parcel volume has actually fallen dramatically—from 725 million parcels in 1968 to 203 million in 1979. This volume decline results in higher processing costs for each parcel, and these higher unit costs in turn lead to higher parcel post rates, and subsequently still more volume loss. Thus, the Postal Service's parcel operation is caught in a cycle of cumulative deterioration. This is one of the main reasons why the rate of return on the $1 billion capital investment in the Bulk Mail System—originally expected to be 33 per cent—now is estimated to be less than 4 per cent, an annual savings of only $40 million instead of the $330 million earlier expected.[36]

Increasing the Efficiency of Delivery

In an effort to control costs, the Postal Service has focused not only on mail-processing methods inside postal facilities but also on the cost of delivery operations. The delivery function commands special attention from postal management because the number of delivery points, or addresses, continues to grow by more than 1.5 million each year, and delivery-service costs account for about 28 per cent of the system's total costs. Most of this cost is an institutional cost—that is, a cost incurred simply by putting the letter carriers on the street, regardless of how much mail they are carrying. The principal determinants of delivery service costs are mode of delivery (whether to the door, to a curbside box, and so on) and frequency of delivery (now six days a week). But the Postal Service has experienced serious obstacles in three of its main efforts to control delivery costs: (1) instituting new forms of delivery in residential areas; (2) redrawing carrier routes to increase efficiency; and (3) eliminating Saturday deliveries.

Residential Deliveries

For years it has been evident to postal management that the proliferation of sprawling new suburban communities would quickly stretch postal manpower and costs beyond limits if letter carriers had to deliver mail to the doorsteps. Thus in the mid-1960s the old Post Office Department directed local offices to provide curbside delivery to all new service areas. But citizens and housing developers across the country disliked the new policy and made their views known to Congress. Elderly and handicapped residents worried about getting out to the curb to retrieve their mail. And Larry Blackmon, the president of the National Association of Homebuilders, described the postal department's move as a "step backward," calling it inconsistent with the efforts of the Johnson Administration to beautify and improve city and suburban environments. Blackmon said: "Rows of curbline mail boxes detract from the beauty of these areas, whether the mailboxes are of uniform or mixed design." [37] Pressed by the public and by groups such as Blackmon's, several congressmen introduced legislation to require the Post Office Department to provide delivery to the door in residential communities. The postmaster general finally backed down in the face of gathering opposition to this cost-saving measure and opened the way for door service to more than 4 million homes that would have been affected by the ban.

After the Post Office Department was reconstituted in its more independent form, Postal Service executives once again explored alternatives to door delivery in residential areas, especially suburbs. Postal officials determined that the Service could save $210 million annually by replacing door delivery whenever possible with curbside or cluster-box delivery. (A "cluster box" is a centralized unit, with anywhere from 18 to 100 lockboxes, to which all the mail for a given neighborhood is delivered.) Whereas the average annual cost of door delivery in the early 1970s was $49 a household, curbside delivery cost the Postal Service only $39 annually, and delivery to a cluster box cut the cost still further—to $24.[38]

With this potential saving in view, the Postal Service in 1972 established a policy that would make almost all new housing developments ineligible for door-to-door delivery. For new residential housing areas, the policy limited the delivery options to curbside service or lockbox service at a cluster box located within 300 feet of the residence. The only circumstances under which the local post office could provide door delivery were for residences built to fill in an area already receiving door delivery and for extreme hardship cases (handicapped or elderly persons, for example); the exceptions had to be approved by the regional postmaster general.[39]

Once again, the National Association of Home Builders (claiming to be worried about "discrimination against persons who buy homes in a new area"), community associations, irate owners of new homes, and persons alarmed by the potentially negative aesthetic effects of the regulations flooded Congress with complaints over the new policy.[40] Residents of some California communities complained that they had been working for years to improve the appearance of their towns by placing telephone and power lines underground, eliminating all poles and wires from the streets, only to be faced now with sprouting cluster boxes.

Congress quickly acted to block the policy's application. Through amendments in 1976 to the Postal Reorganization Act, Congress directed the Postal Service to provide (depending on the average dimensions of the lots in a new development) either door delivery or curbside delivery to all new residential addresses. The Postal Service followed the congressional instructions, but complained that this constraint "reduced the efficiency of delivery management."[41]

Carrier Route Evaluation

Another effort by postal management to trim costs and increase the efficiency of delivery services involved the testing of a new system in 1974 for making the best use of letter carriers' time on the street. Before 1974, local supervisors conducted one-week mail counts for each route and also accompanied each carrier on his or her route to evaluate the carrier's performance and to determine the amount of time necessary to perform various street functions. After the mail count and route inspections, the supervisor determined whether the routes should be adjusted or left alone; but there were few good guidelines for making that decision.

The designers of the new system—the Letter Carrier Route Evaluation System (LCRES)—tried to reduce what higher managers felt was the subjectivity of the earlier route evaluation. Under LCRES, the supervisor of a carrier station, accompanied by efficiency experts from Washington, would measure the total distance traveled on each block of the station's carrier routes, noting the number of mailboxes served, stairs climbed, doors or gates opened and closed, collection boxes served, and so forth. The route evaluators would then enter all this information for each route (along with the data from a two-week mail volume count) in a computer, which would use standards derived from time and motion studies to establish the amount of time needed to serve each block in the area covered by that carrier station.[42] The LCRES computer would also provide the station supervisor with statistical information on which he could base the number of routes that should be established for the station. The supervisor, after deciding how many routes to establish, would design new routes by determining what blocks could sensibly be put together as a route and then extracting from the computer the time value of each block. He would follow this process until a set of eight-hour routes had been developed. Correctly performed, these procedures would theoretically result in the design of efficient and equitable eight-hour routes.[43]

The first test of the new system occurred in Kokomo, Indiana, in 1974, at the South Kokomo carrier station. (Consequently, the program came to be more popularly known as the "Kokomo Plan.") Before the test, this station had 25 regular carrier routes. Following initial measurements, the number fell to 22 regular routes and one part-time route. After further analysis early in 1975, the number of routes increased to 23 regular and one part-time.[44]

James Braughton, director of the Delivery Service Department at postal headquarters, encouraged by the results of the initial Kokomo study, announced a plan to evaluate 1,013 routes in post offices around the country. Braughton's department was trying at this stage to determine what effect LCRES might have if it were fully implemented nationwide. The Postal Service hoped the system could eventually save $425 million a year in labor costs. The designers of LCRES expected it to improve letter-carrier efficiency so much that 25,000 of the postal system's 200,000 carrier jobs could be eliminated.[45]

The reaction from the National Association of Letter Carriers was swift and sharp. Fearing massive future job losses if the program were installed nationwide, the union charged that LCRES would neither increase carrier efficiency nor save money since it would lead to excessive overtime, that the plan was not "fair, reasonable, and equitable," as required by the labor contract, and that the "trivial" changes in routes produced by the system could well lead to worsened service for mail recipients.[46] The union took the issue to arbitration in an effort to block full use of the evaluation plan.

Heeding the growing controversy over the plan, postal executives began to speak out on the subject. "At stake in the LCRES issue," Postmaster General Benjamin Bailar told assembled field managers in March 1975, "is management's right and obligation to test and implement programs that will lead to a more efficient way of processing and delivering the mail." Bailar's senior assistant for employee and labor relations, Darrell F. Brown, said of the union opposition:[47]

> We are not backing off this test program just because the NALC threatens an illegal strike. We all know that the Postal Service's national agreement [with the unions] has a no-layoff provision and that this provision will be honored. There is, therefore, no truth to the speculation that we will be laying off thousands of letter carriers. . . . We have a right to test programs like this. The right of management to run this business cannot be given up.

But on August 10, 1976, labor arbiter Sylvester Garrett ordered the Postal Service to abandon the LCRES plan and to reinstate the old routes used before the testing began in Kokomo and in Portland, Oregon.[48]

Cutting Frequency of Deliveries

The Postal Service faced a successful challenge from the letter carriers on yet another of its plans to cut the costs of delivery operations—reducing the frequency of deliveries. Market research conducted by the Postal Service has shown that the organization could satisfy the demands of over 90 per cent of its present customers with only three-day-a-week delivery.[49] But when the Postal Service has tried to take even modest steps in this direction, strong opposition has arisen to block its efforts. For example, in May 1977, the Postal Service declared its intention of eliminating Saturday deliveries—a move that reportedly would have saved over $400 million a year.[50] The Postal Service decided to go ahead with the plan after an A. C. Nielsen Co. poll, conducted for a postal study commission, found that 79 per cent of the public would be willing to forgo the sixth delivery day if such a move would help hold down the rate of increase in postal rates (its proponents claimed it would).[51]

But the postal employee unions (particularly the letter carriers' organization) feared that eliminating Saturday delivery would lead to eventual reductions in the postal workforce and a corresponding decline in union membership. Officers of the National Association of Letter Carriers, announcing that their union would "do everything in our power—use every means available to make sure that five-day delivery never becomes a reality," persuaded Congressman Charles Wilson (Democrat from California and chairman of a House postal subcommittee) to introduce in the House of Representatives a concurrent resolution that six-day delivery be retained.[52] The vigor with which the union expressed its feelings on the matter showed through in the final outcome; the House overwhelmingly passed the Wilson resolution in late September 1977 by a vote of 377 to 9.[53] Though the resolution had no force of law, it was enough to dissuade the Postal Service from pressing ahead with its plan.

Another celebrated attempt by the Postal Service to cut operating costs, which would have involved reducing and rationalizing its network of post offices, elicited staunch opposition from postmasters, members of Congress, and the Postal Rate Commission.

Trimming the Network of Post Offices

Besides trying to cut costs in mail processing and delivery, the Postal Service has also focused attention on a third important determinant of postal costs, namely, the network of post offices across the United States. The Postal Service in 1979 operated over 30,000 post offices, branches, and stations—a network that has been gradually diminishing in size ever since 1901, when the number peaked at 76,945. Though thousands of small, uneconomical post offices have been closed over the years, thousands still remain. Yet, the Postal Service faces sharp constraints on its ability to prune the postal system of these facilities.

One important limitation was imposed by Congress when it passed the Postal Reorganization Act in 1970. Some legislators were worried that a business-minded postal corporation might be overzealous in its efforts at economy, so the act contains language that clarifies the congressional intent on post office closings:[54]

> *The Postal Service shall provide a maximum degree of effective and regular postal services to rural areas, communities, and small towns where post offices are not self-sustaining. No small post office shall be closed solely for operating at a deficit, it being the specific intent of the Congress that effective postal services be insured to residents of both urban and rural communities.*

Thus, when the Postal Service has closed rural offices, it has argued that the closings are not inconsistent with this statutory direction, since the Service ensures "effective postal services" to the affected communities through well-equipped rural carriers who are "traveling post offices," selling stamps, accepting packages, registering mail, and so forth.

Even so, the Postal Service has found its efforts in this regard vigorously opposed by its own managers (postmasters concerned about their jobs), by members of Congress, and by persons in the affected communities who argue that small rural post offices are the social heartbeat of isolated communities, gathering places for the exchange of news, and centers for the nourishment of local identities. To these people, post office closings threaten to destroy the social fabric of life in rural areas. This array of opposition has guaranteed predictably lively controversies over post office closings.

In the first four years after the reorganization, there was little concern on anyone's part, because the new Postal Service was closing post offices at no higher rate than the old Post Office Department had—roughly 300 offices a year. But a controversy arose in 1975 when the General Accounting Office issued a report contending that if the Postal Service closed down 12,000 small rural post offices, $100 million could be saved annually without diminishing the quality of postal services in the affected areas.[55] The report added fuel to the Postal Service's efforts to cut the system's operating costs, and the Service took advantage of the publicity surrounding the report to build support for more closings. It publicized, for example, the facts about three offices that it had recently closed, indicating that they were typical of most such offices.[56] The data are shown in the accompanying table.

Drum, Kentucky	
Families served	None (even the postmaster's mail was delivered by rural carrier)
Annual receipts	$105
Annual costs	$3,801
Nearest P.O.	Ruth, only 6 miles away
Rosebud, Illinois	
Families served	Six
Annual receipts	$573
Annual costs	$5,587
Nearest P.O.	Brownfield, only 4 miles away
Kelly, Georgia	
Families served	Sixteen
Annual receipts	$1,802
Annual costs	$7,337
Nearest P.O.	Shady Grove, only 3.7 miles away

But the Postal Service effort to build support for cutting costs backfired. Rural postmasters' rising concern over their job prospects, combined with the negative publicity that seemed to cast all rural post offices in a bad light, prompted the National League of Postmasters to fight back. Arguing that an annual savings of $100 million would be inconsequential in view of the Postal Service's enormous budget (then about $13.5 billion), and that the rural post offices were important to community identity at America's crossroads, the league filed a civil action to stop any policy of increased office closings, and, more important, initiated a massive lobbying effort on Capitol Hill to persuade Congress to intervene.[57]

The Postal Service was fighting a losing battle. The postmasters had a formidable lobbying organization. In addition, the Postal Service would have difficulty convincing any given congressman that closing one or more post offices in his district was essential to the fiscal integrity of the Postal Service. The congressional attitude, understandably, was that surely the Postal Service could find other ways of economizing. Moreover, the office-closing fight was taking place just as the bad news about the bulk-mail system was beginning to appear. At hearings on the closing of post offices, Representative Norman Mineta (Dem., Calif.) evoked laughter from the others present when he sarcastically asked a GAO witness "How long will it take the U.S. Postal Service, using its savings from closing rural post offices, to pay off its losses on the bulk-mail system?" [58]

Some members of Congress clearly thought also that the Postal Service was moving too far toward a business-minded approach to its operations and forgetting its "service" responsibilities. Representative Don Fuqua (Dem., Fla.) told his House colleagues: "I have always felt that the word *service* in the name implies just that. We don't look upon our fire department or our police department or other services to turn a profit. We look at them to provide a service." [59] Similarly, Representative Paul Simon (Dem., Ill.) observed: "The name of the organization is Postal Service and not Postal Money Maker." [60]

Still other members of Congress picked up on the theme that rural post offices serve as informal town halls and community centers, providing a sense of community identity. "The rural post office has always been an uniquely American institution," said Representative Patsy Mink (Dem., Hawaii).[61] And Senator Jennings Randolph (Dem., W. Va.) told his colleagues: "When such offices are closed, the American flag really comes down." [62] Thus, in many legislators' views, efficiency and economy alone were not good enough reasons to close rural post offices.

Congress responded to the postmasters' pleas and to the arguments of individual members of Congress by including a provision in its 1976 amendments to the Postal Reorganization Act, imposing a temporary moratorium against closing or consolidating any post office, and also establishing a permanent procedure under which the Postal Service may close or consolidate a post office only after the citizens of the community have been advised of the plans and have had an opportunity to present their views.[63]

Once the moratorium won by the postmasters was lifted, however, the Postal Service launched a controversial new campaign to weaken local community resistance to post office closings. The Postal Service public relations department began sending out news releases and letters to newspaper editors, disclosing information about the salary of the local postmaster and the annual revenues of the post office. Many newspapers made feature stories of the information. The Baltimore *Sun*, for example, published the salaries of every postmaster in the state, informing the paper's readers statewide about postmaster salaries in Maryland communities such as Girdletree (G. B. Jones, $17,004) and Church Creek (F. E. Fitzhugh, $16,499).[64] Many postmasters across the country were angry over this tactic of the Postal Service because, as Frank Miklozek, executive director of the National Association of Postmasters, charged, the policy appeared to have been designed to create resentment against the postmasters (many of whom were better paid than most other town residents) and to soften community resistance to post office closings. "If a postmaster's salary is published, people in the town who make less money are bound to feel resentful," Miklozek explained to a reporter in 1977.[65] The Postal Service innocently proclaimed that the information campaign was merely an attempt "to show how important the Postal Service is to the local economy."[66]

The Postal Service encountered yet another hurdle in trying to cut costs; this was the intervention by the Postal Rate Commission (PRC), the agency Congress established at the time of the postal reorganization to review proposed changes in postal rates and services. In judging appeals on closings or consolidations of offices, the PRC has a function analogous to that of a U.S. Court of Appeals entertaining a petition for review of an administrative agency's action. Like those courts, the PRC is restricted in these cases to reviewing the administrative record made by the agency; it is not free to conduct its own fact-finding investigations or hearings. When the Postal Service tried in 1979 to close 90 small post offices and replace them with alternative forms of service, 21 of those closings were appealed to the PRC. The commission remanded all 21 cases to the Postal Service, insisting that the Postal Service had not given enough attention to the congressional instruction that it consider "the effect on the community" of closing a post office. The PRC believed in particular that the Postal Service was not considering effects unrelated to mail service, even though the legislative history of the 1976 amendment clearly showed that its sponsors were at least as concerned with preserving the economic and social benefits of local post offices as with ensuring satisfactory mail service. The rate commission criticized the Postal Service for acting too much as the prudent manager of its own operations and not enough as a guardian of the public interest.[67]

Because of all these constraints, in the entire period between 1976 and 1979, the Postal Service closed only 72 offices, reducing its network from 30,521 to 30,449.[68] The Postal Service's difficulties in pruning its network of small, costly offices contrasts sharply with the experience of many private firms that have multiple outlets. The case of the Great Atlantic and Pacific Tea Company (A&P), one of the nation's largest supermarket chains, is instructive.

In early 1979, A&P announced the closing of 174 of its retail outlets in the Midwest and Northeast. This accounted for 10 per cent of the firm's entire network of 1,634 stores. A company vice president explained that although A&P regretted having to close the stores, "the cost of continuing to keep them open . . . seriously hampered our company's efforts to sustain profitable operations." [69] That was that. The employees in the A&P stores closed by the management decision did not appear on Capitol Hill asking Congress to block the closings. Nor did inconvenienced citizens agitate in hopes of persuading Congress to reverse the decision. But even if all this had happened, there is little Congress could have done to force A&P to keep those stores open.

The Postal Service situation is obviously quite different. The willingness of Congress to accede to the demands of organized interests hinders Postal Service efforts to achieve the productivity improvements and economies gained by many private sector service industries over the past quarter century. The supermarket itself is an example of such an improvement; it represents a substantial increase in productivity over the old corner grocery store where the clerk filled orders for waiting customers. The advent of the supermarket ended this slow, inefficient mode of operation and substituted it with fast and efficient self-service operations in which the customer is made to cooperate in the production process.[70] Along the same lines, once food distributors learned the economics of the supermarket, old services such as home delivery of milk, eggs, and bakery products largely went the way of the corner grocery store.

Anyone who wonders why the Postal Service remains costly and "inefficient" need only imagine the public outcries and political obstacles postal executives would face if they tried to end home delivery of mail and replace it with delivery to centralized mail lockbox stations, perhaps located next to the supermarket in local shopping centers. Dairy farms and dry cleaners can get away with such economizing measures; governmental organizations cannot. Indeed, as we have seen, the Postal Service even has trouble getting suburban residents to agree to walk out to their front curbline to receive their mail.

Summary

The Postal Service has undertaken numerous efforts over the past decade to control costs and improve operating efficiency. The results of these efforts are largely discouraging. The Postal Service today may appear to be a less labor-intensive operation than the Post Office of 1970 since more mail is now machine-processed, more carrier routes are motorized, and fewer employees are on the payroll. But it is only an illusion. In reality, 86 per cent of all postal costs in 1979 were labor costs—a much higher percentage than the 80 per cent that postal reformers bemoaned in 1970. Moreover, productivity gains during this period have been relatively meager despite a 3.6 per cent increase each year since 1972 in the supervisory and technical workforce.

.The problem here, of course, is that many of postal management's concentrated efforts to control costs and improve productivity have been blocked by the effective opposition of politically influential outside interests and by the determined resistance of the powerful postal employee unions. And when the Postal Service *has* succeeded in putting through progams to increase productivity (with mechanization, say) or to restrain the rate of increase in operating costs (by the hiring freeze), that success has come at the price of deterioration in service. This is hardly an attractive trade-off for the Postal Service because politically it is a no-win situation.

Most frustrating of all to postal management is that the cost of personnel compensation and benefits has increased so much that any beneficial consequences of increased productivity have been outweighed. For example, although the number of pieces of mail handled per man-year increased approximately 22 per cent between 1971 and 1978, the number of pieces handled per constant dollar of personnel wages and benefits declined approximately 3 per cent.[71]

Some of this problem is the result of extraordinarily high inflation during the 1970s. But as we shall see, the increased costs of employee compensation and benefits (without corresponding productivity improvements) are also the result of the enhanced strategic position held by the postal unions under the collective bargaining process that the Postal Reorganization Act established.

Endnotes

1. U.S. Postal Service, *Annual Report of the Postmaster General, 1979,* pp. 24, 27.
2. U.S. Post Office Department, *Annual Report of the Postmaster General, Fiscal 1969* (Washington: U.S. Government Printing Office, 1969), p. 241.
3. Commission on Postal Service, *Report of the Commission on Postal Service* (Washington: U.S. Government Printing Office, 1977), vol. 1, p. 15.
4. See Carl H. Scheele, *A Short History of the Mail Service* (Washington: Smithsonian Institution Press, 1976), pp. 92–97, 103–105, 169–170, 175–177, 185–186.
5. Dan Cordtz, "It's Now or Never for the Post Office," *Fortune,* March 1967, p. 136.
6. President's Commission on Postal Organization, Report of the Commission, *Towards Postal Excellence* (Washington: U.S. Government Printing Office, 1968), pp. 25–27, 35.
7. Cordtz, "Now or Never," p. 136.
8. Maurice B. Feimster, quoted in *Newsweek,* July 13, 1959, p. 23.
9. U.S. Postal Service, General Release No. 28, March 29, 1972.
10. *New York Times,* August 29, 1972, p. 1
11. *New York Times,* February 18, 1973, p. 1.
12. See, for example, U.S. Congress, House, Committee on Post Office and Civil Service, *Status and Performance of the U.S. Postal Service, Hearings before a Subcommittee of the Committee on Post Office and Civil Service,* 93rd Cong., 1st Sess., 1973.
13. From statement of Morris Biller, president of the Manhattan-Bronx Postal Union, in U.S., Congress, House, Committee on Post Office and Civil Service, *Oversight Hearings on the Postal Service, Hearings before a Subcommittee of the Committee on Post Office and Civil Service,* 93rd Cong., 1st Sess., 1973, p. 243.

14. E. V. Dorsey, senior assistant postmaster general for operations, testimony in *ibid.*, p. 272.

15. U.S., Congress, Senate, Committee on Post Office and Civil Service, *Postal Oversight, Hearings before the Committee on Post Office and Civil Service,* 93rd Cong., 1st Sess., 1973, p. 68.

16. U.S. Postal Service, *Annual Report of the Postmaster General, 1973–1974,* p. 47.

17. Some observers consider the Zip Code one of the greatest improvements in the postal system in recent years. In an informal sampling of senior postal employees, Matthew Bowyer asked respondents to state what, in their opinion, were the greatest boons to the Post Office between 1940 and 1970. The top two answers: Zip Code and a 1968 directive that permitted letter packets to be held together with rubber bands instead of tied with jute twine, the practice for over 100 years. Matthew Bowyer, *They Carried the Mail* (New York: Robert B. Luce, 1972), p. 69.

18. The Postal Service has begun to revise and expand the Zip Code, planning to add four more digits to the present five-digit code. The additional digits will permit sorting to carrier routes and even to individual city blocks, thereby reducing delivery errors, handling time, and costs (*New York Times,* May 20, 1979, p. H2).

19. This description of postal mechanization is based on personal observation and on the simple, accurate description in Joseph Albright, "U.S. Mail: Ziptronic, but Zipless," *New York Times Magazine,* February 2, 1975, p. 26.

20. *Ibid.,* p. 10.

21. For more on the area mail-processing program, see U.S., Congress, House, Committee on Post Office and Civil Service, *Continuity of Management—U.S. Postal Service, Hearings before a Subcommittee of the Committee on Post Office and Civil Service,* 93rd Cong., 2d Sess., 1974, pp. 160–167; and U.S. Congress, House, Committee on Post Office and Civil Service, *Briefing by the Postmaster General, Joint Hearings before the Subcommittee of the Committee on Post Office and Civil Service,* 93rd Cong., 1st Sess., 1973, pp. 39–41.

22. Concerning misdirected mail and the delays and increased costs it creates, see Comptroller General of the United States, *Missent Mail—A Contributing Factor to Mail Delay and Increased Costs,* report to the Congress (Washington: General Accounting Office, October 27, 1974), esp. p. 6.

23. U.S. Postal Service, *Comprehensive Statement on Postal Operations,* January 1980, p. 28.

24. *New York Times,* May 20, 1979, p. H2.

25. U.S. Postal Service, General Release No. 29, March 11, 1971. Blount's "assembly line" comment is quoted in the *Washington Post,* June 12, 1974, p. A8.

26. U.S., Congress, House, Committee on Appropriations, *Treasury, Postal Service, and General Government Appropriations for Fiscal Year 1973, Hearings before a Subcommittee of the Committee on Appropriations,* 92d Cong., 2d Sess., 1973, p. 29.

27. Postal Inspection Service report, quoted in Comptroller General of the United States, *Problems of the New National Bulk Mail System,* report to the Congress (Washington: General Accounting Office, December 10, 1976), #GGD-76-100, p. 19.

28. U.S., Congress, House, Committee on Post Office and Civil Service, *National Bulk Mail System, Hearings before a Subcommittee of the Committee on Post Office and Civil Service,* 94th Cong., 2d Sess., 1976, pp. 11, 18; also pp. 54, 58.

29. GAO Report, *Problems of the New National Bulk Mail System,* p. 19; and Comptroller General of the United States, *Grim Outlook for the United States Postal Service's National Bulk Mail System,* report to the Congress (Washington: General Accounting Office, May 16, 1978), #GGD-78-59, p. 17.

30. GAO Report, *Grim Outlook,* p. 17.

31. U.S. Postal Service, *The Report of the Joint Industry/Postal Service Alternative Delivery Task Force,* March 1979, Volume 2, p. 31.

32. GAO Report, *Problems of the New National Bulk Mail System,* p. 15.

33. GAO Report, *Grim Outlook,* p. 20.

34. *Ibid.,* pp. 14.

35. *Ibid.,* pp. 15, 43.

36. *Ibid.,* p. 30

37. *Washington Post,* May 21, 1966, p. F3.

38. Comptroller General of the United States, letter report to Senator Alan Cranston (#GGD-75-92), June 9, 1975, p. 3.

39. *Postal Leader,* November 1972, p. 1.

40. U.S., Congress, Senate, Committee on Post Office and Civil Service, *Postal Reorganization, Hearings before the Committee on Post Office and Civil Service,* 94th Cong., 2d Sess., 1976, pp. 304–306.

41. U.S., Congress, House, Committee on Post Office and Civil Service, *General Oversight and Postal Service Budget, Hearings before a Subcommittee of the Committee on Post Office and Civil Service,* 95th Cong., 1st Sess., 1977, pp. 48, 49.

42. The basis for the new standards was the method-time-measurement (MTM) system. Under this system:

> *Each motion that an individual must use to perform a work function has a predetermined time value. The values for these motions are accumulated into a composite standard for a work function. For example, there may be 15 or 20 motions required to perform a function such as casing a letter. Each function is measured and the total of the values for the various movements becomes the standard for casing a letter. Such standards have been developed for all office and street activities. These predetermined values represent a person working at a normal rate and are based on thousands of observations.*

From statement of James Braughton, director of the U.S. Postal Service's Delivery Services Department, quoted in *Postal Leader,* May 1975, p. 5.

43. Ibid.

44. *Ibid.,* p. 1.

45. *Postal Leader,* April 1975, p. 5.

46. *New York Times,* February 7, 1975, p. 10.

47. *Postal Leader,* April 1975, p. 5.

48. *Wall Street Journal,* August 11, 1976, p. 3.

49. U.S., Congress, House, Committee on Post Office and Civil Service, *Postal*

Service Staff Study: "The Necessity for Change," Committee Print No. 94-26, 94th Cong., 2d Sess., 1976, p. 37.

50. *Washington Star,* May 16, 1977, p. 1.
51. Commission on Postal Service, *Report of the Commission on Postal Service,* vol. 1, p. 50.
52. *Postal Record,* May 1977, p. 4.
53. *Washington Post,* September 27, 1977, p. A3.
54. *United States Code,* Title 39, sec. 101(b).
55. Comptroller General of the United States, *$100 Million Could Be Saved Annually in Postal Operations in Rural America without Affecting the Quality of Service,* report to the Congress (Washington: General Accounting Office, June 4, 1975), #GGD-75-87.
56. For one appearance of this information, see National League of Postmasters, *Postmasters Advocate Weekly,* July 30, 1976, p. 1.
57. *Ibid.*
58. U.S., Congress, House, Committee on Post Office and Civil Service, *GAO's Recommendations That 12,000 Small Post Offices Be Closed, Joint Hearings before the Subcommittees on Postal Service and Postal Facilities, Mail, and Labor Management of the Committee on Post Office and Civil Service,* 94th Cong., 1st Sess., 1975, p. 40.
59. U.S., Congress, House, Committee on Post Office and Civil Service, *Cutbacks in Postal Service, Hearings before the Subcommittee on Postal Service of the Committee on Post Office and Civil Service,* 94th Cong., 2d Sess., 1976, p. 15.
60. U.S., Congress, GAOs *Recommendations That 12,000 Small Post Offices Be Closed, Hearings,* p. 20.
61. *Ibid.,* pp. 4–5.
62. U.S., Congress, House, Committee on Post Office and Civil Service, *H.R. 8603, Postal Reorganization Act Amendments of 1976, Legislative History,* Committee Print No. 94-20, 94th Cong., 2d Sess., 1976, p. 336. This and several of the preceding quotes came to my attention in Robert D. Behn, "Closing a Government Facility," *Public Administration Review* (July/August, 1978), vol. 38, no. 4, p. 333.
63. *United States Code,* Title 39, sec. 404(b).
64. *The Sun* (Baltimore), September 11, 1977, pp. B1, B2.
65. *Washington Star,* June 1, 1977, p. A12.
66. *Ibid.*
67. U.S., Postal Rate Commission, *Commission Opinion Remanding Determinations for Further Consideration,* Docket Nos. A79-1 through A79-9 (Washington: Postal Rate Commission, May 7, 1979), pp. 1, 3, 4, 16; Docket Nos. A79-10 through A79-21 (Washington: Postal Rate Commission, July 20, 1979), p. 1.
68. U.S. Postal Service, *Annual Report of the Postmaster General, Fiscal 1979,* p. 31.
69. John B. Kienke, vice president of A&P's Boston division, quoted in *Boston Globe,* March 25, 1979, p. 47.
70. See Theodore Levitt, "Management and the 'Post-Industrial' Society," *Public Interest,* no. 44 (1976), p. 85.
71. U.S. Postal Service, *Annual Report of the Postmaster General, Fiscal 1978,* p. 9.

Chapter 4

POSTAL UNIONS AND COLLECTIVE BARGAINING

Few elements of postal policymaking have undergone greater change as a result of the 1970 reorganization than labor-management relations, particularly the procedures and institutional arrangements for setting the wages and benefits of the postal system's 600,000 rank-and-file employees. The Postal Reorganization Act inaugurated direct collective bargaining between Postal Service management and the postal unions. This change, revolutionary for the federal government, sought to take "politics" out of postal wage and benefit determination by removing the process from the legislative arena. Reformers hoped, moreover, that if postal management had a more direct role in determining the compensation levels of postal workers, it could reduce the percentage of the system's total costs accounted for by labor costs.

Though the changes wrought by the reorganization have succeeded in reducing the part that elected officials have in determining postal wages, they have by no means taken politics or conflict out of wage setting. If anything, controversies over postal wages have increased as the stakes have become greater. The reorganization has also caused a newly bitter, adversary relation to be set between postal management and the employee unions. Finally, collective bargaining has failed to increase management's ability to control labor costs. If anything, it has conspicuously strengthened the hand of the postal unions in dealing with management, and has (at least so far) enhanced union ability to extract favorable compensation increases for postal workers.

79

The Rise of the Unions as a Political Force

The history of postal labor-management relations is unusually long
and rich, since postal employees were the first federal employees to
join unions in significant numbers. Though skilled craftsmen working in the shipyards of the U.S. Navy and in the U.S. Government
Printing Office had organized earlier in the nineteenth century, it
was in the nation's post offices that federal employee unionism
caught hold and grew.[1]

For most of the nineteenth century, favoritism and partisanship
dominated the postal personnel system. Postmasters and supervisors
typically were prominent local politicians. Local post offices were
managed as if they were "adjuncts of the local political machine of
the party nationally in power." [2] In those days, an individual ac-
quired a postal job through partisan ties and lost it when there was
a local or national change in party or even in faction. But for as
long as the postal worker held the job, he was expected to lend active support to the party organization. A failure to live up to that
expectation might result in extra work, a reduction in pay, or even
dismissal. The postal worker had, moreover, no legal protection
from this sort of treatment, since working conditions (including
hours of work and pay) were fixed not by law but by the local postmaster, who paid the employees in his office whatever he liked from
the lump-sum appropriation given him by the Post Office Department. Local postal officials had particular friends and supporters
who received the best jobs and the best pay. But no employee was
secure in either his pay or his job, for if something untoward happened to his well-placed friend, something bad was likely to hap-
pen to him also.[3] This system subjected employees to extraordinarily capricious and arbitrary treatment and led to gross inequities
within individual post offices as well as throughout the postal system.

Organized efforts by postal employees to change this situation
did not emerge until the 1880s. Until then there simply had not
been a great enough incentive; for most postal workers, hope for
improvement in their lot rested not with concerted action but with
individual political pull.

Congressional passage in 1883 of the Civil Service Act—intended
to eliminate the most egregious political abuses of postal employ-

ment at the local and national levels—changed the picture. As the patronage value of postal positions gradually disappeared after 1883, congressmen and other politicians began to lose interest in the postal clerks and letter carriers. And without their former patrons, these workers soon found it necessary to unite among themselves to protect their interests and improve their situations. With their positions made permanent by the tenure provision of the civil service act, postal employees came to recognize that they had a stake in the service and in good working conditions. The organized labor movement among postal employees was the logical result of these developments.[4]

The city letter carriers were the first postal employees to unite for concerted action, forming the National Association of Letter Carriers in 1889. A year later, the postal clerks also established a national association. And by 1908, the rural letter carriers, the postmasters, and the postal supervisors had created associations too.[5]

Once established however, the postal employee organizations encountered many obstacles, most placed in their way by unsympathetic or openly antagonistic postal officials in Washington. In 1895, for instance, Postmaster General William L. Wilson, annoyed by the increasing political activity of the employee organizations both in the Capitol and at the department, issued an order prohibiting any postal employee from visiting Washington, whether on leave with or without pay, for the purpose of influencing legislation before Congress. Wilson's order explained his position this way:[6]

> *Postmasters and other employees of the Postal Service are paid by the Government for attending to the respective duties assigned them, which do not include efforts to secure legislation. That duty is assigned to the representatives of the people elected for that purpose.*
>
> *If bills are introduced in either branch of Congress affecting the Postal Service, upon which any information or recommendation is desired, I am ready at all times to submit such as lies within my power and province.*

This was the first of a series of attempts to limit by official regulation the activities of postal employees in their own behalf. But the rule was poorly enforced and thus widely ignored.

When in 1901 the House Committee on Post Office and Post Roads had before it important bills affecting both clerks and letter carriers, the associations representing these employees lobbied vigorously and untiringly on Capitol Hill, deluging President Theodore Roosevelt with telegrams, letters, and petitions. Roosevelt, whether urged on by Eugene F. Lord, chairman of the committee, or acting out of his own annoyance or conviction that the employees' activities were inappropriate, on January 31, 1902, issued the first of his famous "gag orders:" [7]

> *All officers and employees of the United States of every description, serving in or under any of the Executive Departments, and whether so serving in or out of Washington, are hereby forbidden, either directly or indirectly, individually or through associations, to solicit an increase of pay or to influence or attempt to influence in their own interest any other legislation whatever either before Congress or its Committees, or in any way save through the heads of the Departments in or under which they serve, on penalty of dismissal from the Government service.*

The gag order remained in force for a full decade, but finally was lifted when the Lloyd-LaFollette Act was passed in 1912. This statute recognized the right of federal civil servants to form associations for promoting their own welfare and to affiliate with outside labor organizations, so long as these organizations did not assert the right of public employees to strike against the government. The act furthermore granted federal employees the right to lobby and petition Congress. This last provision proved especially important in the years to come as the postal labor organizations, periodically confronted by hostile postmasters general, forged close and mutually beneficial ties with members of Congress.[8]

Postal Union Influence with Congress

The unions, established to provide a political presence representing the interests of postal workers, laid special emphasis over the years on cultivating good relations with members of Congress, especially those who sat on the post office committees. All important postal staff and labor decisions—wage schedule, classification of positions, conditions of job security, and even details of work assignments— were determined by Congress (the House Post Office and Civil Service Committee, in particular) through prolonged tripartite bargaining with the Post Office Department and the postal unions. Over the years, the postal unions became expert at lobbying Congress, and they came to these deliberations with unusual political strength, derived from a combination of resources, most of which they still possess today.

First, the unions enjoyed the advantage of large size and wide geographic distribution. At the time of the reorganization, the combined membership of the various postal unions totaled almost 600,000. The Post Office Department was (like its successor) the most highly unionized federal organization. Among letter carriers, for example, 98 per cent of those on active duty in 1967 belonged to the National Association of Letter Carriers, and 92 per cent of rural carriers belonged to their union. In all, 90 per cent of postal employees belonged to a union, compared with only 21 per cent in other federal agencies.[9] These figures are important, not only because the remarkably high membership rates provided union leaders with substantial resources and unusual credibility but because the vast legions of organized postal workers constituted a formidable electoral force throughout every congressional district. Supplementing the force of the 600,000 union members were the families and friends of postal employees, who might also be influenced to vote for legislators sympathetic to union interests or oppose those who were not. The postal employees also derived power from congressmen's recognition that unlike most other federal employees postal workers (and letter carriers in particular) have almost daily contact with the public.

Second, the unions were the oldest and strongest of federal employee organizations and had over the years constructed formidable organizations in Washington with full-time staffs to refine and express positions, marshal information, and keep tabs on supporters and opponents.

Third, the postal unions had the advantage of being able to pursue their interests in Washington without any organized opponents. In a city that has organized forces on both sides of almost any issue, the postal unions were among those fortunate groups having no direct, active opponents. The other powerful interest groups in the postal policy arena were the organizations representing the mailing industries—the magazine publishers, direct-mail advertisers, and large mail-order companies. But before the reorganization, there was no basic policy conflict between these two chief blocs. Since the Post Office Department's funding came through appropriations, postal costs and revenues were not directly linked. Therefore an increase in postal employee wages did not necessarily mean an increase in postage rates. Consequently, the unions and the large mailers' associations were seldom inclined to assume antagonistic positions. Indeed, so muted were any policy conflicts between the postal employee unions and the mailers' organizations that for many years, one man, J. Don Kerlin, served both as a lobbyist for a powerful magazine group (Time, Inc.) and as a paid consultant for the National Association of Letter Carriers.[10] If the postal unions can be said to have had any adversary at all it was the executive branch, which normally opposed pay raises or proposed smaller increases than the employee groups wanted.

Fourth, the unions had become highly skilled over the years at what one union official called "the gentle art of lobbying"—placing their organizational strength and financial resources at the disposal of congressional friends and withholding it from (or using it to the detriment of) legislators who proved unsupportive.[11] The unions would, for example, organize testimonial dinners for friendly legislators to help raise money for them. And although the Hatch Act prohibited postal workers from direct involvement in political campaigning, it did not apply to their spouses. Thus, highly influential auxiliary organizations emerged. The Ladies Auxiliary of the National Association of Letter Carriers, for instance, regularly provided volunteers to help with typing, writing letters, stuffing envelopes, and similar tasks—the kind for which it is often hardest to secure volunteer help.[12]

This combination of resources and efforts helped the postal unions establish productive working relations with legislators on the post office committees and with others well situated to help them. Since post office committee members had to absorb intense direct pressure from the unions, the committee members adopted a responsive posture, or a "strategic premise," that promoted collective action by committee members and formed the basis for a pattern of committee decisions. The strategic premise on union demands was (as Richard Fenno has described it) "to support maximum pay increases and improvements in benefits for employee groups and . . . to accede to executive branch wishes [only] when, in the judgement of committee members and employee groups, to do otherwise will net employee groups nothing in that Congress." [13]

This strategic premise, along with cultivation by the unions of

other loyal congressional allies, helped to secure numerous spectac-
ular victories for postal employees in the 1950s and 1960s. When,
for instance, House Post Office and Civil Service Committee Chairman Thomas Murray (who, almost alone among committee members, openly decried the strength of the postal unions and regularly
supported the executive branch position on pay bills) refused to act
on a pay measure in 1960, the union supporters on the committee
saved the bill by acquiring the 218 signatures needed to discharge
the bill from committee. They then pushed the bill through the
House (even under the threat of a presidential veto), and led a successful fight to override the veto—one of only two overrides during
the entire Eisenhower administration.[14] This impressive victory resulted from the effective legislative maneuvering by friendly congressmen and from the prodigious lobbying efforts of the postal employee unions in face-to-face contact with individual members of
the House. A Post Office Department executive who observed the
unions at work on this bill (and others like it) said of their effectiveness: "The pressure from the postal employee groups is terrific—
just terrific. They are the best-organized union in the world. When
they want to turn on the heat they are almost unbearable." [15] And
these efforts by the unions produced impressive though not surprising results; only one postal pay bill was defeated on any kind of
vote in the House during the twelve years from 1955 to 1967.[16]

In view of this successful record, and in light of the tremendous
resources and advantages the unions enjoyed in their relations with
the department and Congress, it is not surprising that the postal
unions were more than a little cautious when Postmaster General
Lawrence F. O'Brien unveiled his postal reorganization proposal
in 1967. The unions had painstakingly built up credibility and
influence through years of lobbying on Capitol Hill and were understandably reluctant to trade all that for the uncertain benefit of
bargaining directly with a team of management negotiators sure to
be more stubborn and resistant. But (as we saw in Chapter 1) the
unions eventually gave their support to the reorganization plan
after their strike in 1970 succeeded in extracting a concessionary 14
per cent wage increase from the Nixon Administration.

The Postal Reorganization Act that was passed by Congress that
summer revolutionized postal labor-management relations. The act
provided that the new Postal Service be governed by the National

Labor Relations Act. It further provided that the Postal Service negotiate agreements on wages, benefits, and working conditions through collective bargaining with the labor organizations that held exclusive recognition rights nationwide as of August 12, 1970, the date of the reorganization act's enactment. These unions represented the maintenance employees, special delivery messengers, motor-vehicle employees, postal clerks, letter carriers, mail handlers, and rural letter carriers. And although the law prohibited strikes by postal workers, it provided for fact-finding and binding third-party arbitration if there were disputes or impasses the parties could not resolve themselves. In short, both postal management and the workers faced a whole new framework for the conduct of their relations—a new game, as it were, with new rules and played on a new, unfamiliar field.

Unions Gird for Battle

The unions' struggle in 1969 and 1970 to win a satisfactory pay raise and to shape the reorganization bill more to their liking (the struggle capped by the effective strike in 1970) showed organized postal workers that their power was not limited to lobbying Congress. Indeed, since the unions would continue to enjoy their formidable array of resources, it seemed possible that their power could just as effectively be exerted in their new, direct adversary relationship with postal management. The controversy surrounding postal pay and reorganization legislation had pulled the unions into a more aggressive posture than they had ever assumed before. The successful strike showed the unions what a powerful (though illegal) weapon they possessed, and at the same time it convinced postal management and others of union ability and willingness to demonstrate strength. In short, by 1970, the organized postal workers had come to view themselves as real labor unions rather than as associations of government employees. This attitude was reflected in an important merger that year of several postal workers' associations—a merger intended to increase the unity of postal workers in their forthcoming confrontations with management.

The first stage of the merger came in December 1970, only four months after President Nixon signed the reorganization act. The United Federation of Postal Clerks (UFPC) led the way, initiating a merger with the National Association of Post Office and General Services Maintenance Employees and with the National Federation of Post Office Motor Vehicle Operators. The next month, the National Association of Special Delivery Messengers also signed the merger agreement, bringing the total membership of the four merged unions (all affiliates of the AFL-CIO) to over 200,000, with the UFPC alone contributing some 175,000 of this total.[17]

In March 1971 an even more important breakthrough in the union merger movement occurred. The National Postal Union (NPU) agreed to merge with the new organization. The NPU had split off from the United Federation of Postal Clerks in 1958, and it included among its 70,000 members the nation's largest and most militant local (the 27,000 member Manhattan-Bronx Postal Union). After favorable referenda on the merger and on a new constitution, the American Postal Workers Union (APWU) became a reality and took its place as one of the largest unions in the AFL-CIO.[18]

Including the NPU in the new union was significant for two reasons. It brought the huge membership bloc into the APWU; also, it signaled at least a temporary end to the lengthy organizational division and internal dissension that had torn the ranks of the postal clerks since 1890, when the first organization of postal clerks, the National Association of Post Office Clerks, had been formed. Underlying the long series of bitter splits and cautious alliances among warring factions of clerks was the great variety in clerical duties, ranging from keeping records to selling stamps or operating high-speed letter-sorting machines. What's more, the few promotions to the supervisory ranks historically had been made from the clerical ranks—a situation further exacerbating the jealousies, rivalries, and presence of factions among post office clerks.[19]

The organizational behavior of the letter carriers, on the other hand, has been quite different. Unlike the clerks, most city carriers are engaged in the same kind of work and remain carriers throughout most of their postal careers, often on the same route.[20] This seems to be an important factor in explaining why the National Association of Letter Carriers (NALC) always has been so strong organizationally and financially, so relatively free of internal strife, and so reluctant to join the less stable clerks and other workers in the new APWU.

Though the letter carriers' union entertained the possibility of joining the merger, NALC President James H. Rademacher wanted assurance that such a step would benefit the NALC. Moving to protect the extensive assets the NALC would bring to any merger, Rademacher delared:[21]

> *The NALC has millions of dollars of assets in real estate and insurance which we are not about to turn over to a merged group of unions without something substantial in return. . . . [A]s the oldest and most respected of all unions representing government workers, we do not intend to turn our assets, our membership and our prestige over to any group or groups until we are confident that in so doing, we would be acting in total support of the welfare of our membership.*

The NALC was never convinced that it should merge, and both it and the even more separatist National Rural Letter Carriers Association stayed out of the new APWU. So also did the mail handlers' union, which earlier had merged into the Laborer's International Union of North America.

But the postal unions nevertheless recognized that they shared common goals in negotiating with management over wages, and that some form of unity was necessary to deal with management from strength. Accordingly, the unions established among themselves the Council of American Postal Employees (CAPE) to coordinate their approach in the coming negotiations.

The Character of the Negotiations

To date, the Postal Service and the unions have concluded four collective bargaining agreements under the terms of the reorganization act—in 1971, 1973, 1975, and 1978. Following are thumbnail sketches of the first three sets of negotiations and a more detailed description of the 1978 contract talks, the only case so far in which the negotiations have exhausted the collective-bargaining provisions of the Postal Reorganization Act.

The 1971 Negotiations

On January 20, 1971, management and the unions met for the start of the first comprehensive collective bargaining in the history of federal government labor relations. During that meeting and in subsequent ones, the Council of American Postal Employees (CAPE), represented by Bernard Cushman, the unions' designated chief negotiator, presented more than sixty extensive demands on basic money items and on a comprehensive array of other matters. Management responded in March of 1971 by saying that there was little money available to meet union demands and that the unions therefore had better establish priorities. By midnight on April 19, the end of the ninety-day bargaining period provided for in the act, the unions and management had failed to agree in spite of a last-minute mediating effort by Assistant Secretary of Labor William J. Usery (who had earlier helped to resolve the March 1970 postal strike).[22]

The unions charged that management negotiators "deliberately torpedoed the first phase of negotiations by refusing to make any wage or monetary offers of any kind." Charging management with "callous disregard of the public interest," Bernard Cushman told a press conference:[23]

> *The department [the U.S. Postal Service] wants collective begging, not collective bargaining. If it continues down the road of a grudging and irritable paternalism, the department will destroy the bright promise of collective bargaining and scuttle the Postal Reform Act. [sic].*

The stalemate automatically triggered the fact-finding procedures provided by the Postal Reorganization Act. The procedures required that the director of the Federal Mediation and Conciliation Service provide both parties to the negotiations with a single list of fifteen independent arbitrators from which the unions and management each were to choose one member. These two were then to choose the third member themselves. By May 3, 1971, the panel was set. Its members included Laurence Seibel, a Washington, D.C., attorney, chosen by the unions on the strength of his bargaining experience; Professor Bernard Meltzer of the University of Chicago, chosen by the Postal Service; and Eli Rock, a Philadelphia attorney, who was chosen by the other two and who became panel chairman. The panel members spent all May familiarizing themselves with the various aspects of the bargaining, and finally issued a twenty-page report that made no substantive recommendations to either side, weakly conceding that the problems were many and complex.[24]

By the time agreement finally was reached in July 1971, the statutory procedures had almost been exhausted, falling just short of binding arbitration. The specter of third-party determination led to crisis bargaining that produced a contract in the final hours. The agreement contained a five-step $1,250 wage increase, plus a cost-of-living adjustment of $160 in July of 1972, and a $300 bonus to mark the formal transition of the Post Office Department from a cabinet agency to an independent establishment of the federal government. The agreement also included an important no-layoff clause, which would haunt management in the following years.[25]

The 1973 Negotiations

The second round of negotiations between postal labor and management commenced in April 1973, amid great apprehension over the coming talks. This time management had appeared at the opening session with a list of its own demands, including elimination of the no-layoff clause, elimination of local negotiations, and an increase in the allowable number of part-time workers and casuals.[26] And in a replay of the 1971 negotiations, management responded to union requests for substantial increases in wages and fringe benefits by saying that management needed to hold the line on the system's costs to prevent a postage rate increase.

The Postal Service remained adamant in the early stages, refusing to yield on any important issue. The unions were similarly intransigent. The Postal Service then began issuing press releases to the effect that postal workers had never had it so good. The reports called attention to the attractiveness of postal salaries by citing the long waiting lists around the country for postal jobs.[27] The unions, angered by management's tactic, countered by announcing plans to mobilize massive demonstrations against postal management in Washington and around the country. More important, the unions contacted business organizations heavily reliant on the postal system and told them there was a distinct possibility of a strike on July 21 unless a new contract was signed and ratified by then. The large mailers, in turn, put pressure on postal management, saying that if there was a strike they would seek out permanent alternative methods of getting their material to the public.[28]

Management's position then changed dramatically. Senior Assistant Postmaster General Darrel F. Brown, management's principal representative at the negotiations, yielded on a number of important points, and his public statements stood in sharp contrast to management's earlier posture:[29]

I am impressed with the need and urgency for improvement in labor relations. . . . We shall not abdicate our authority to manage, but we do have an obligation to share many things with the unions . . . . We want our negotiations and the subsequent agreement to be a model for all.

In what many observers have since come to regard as an extraordinary capitulation by postal management, the Postal Service reached an early and generous agreement with the unions. Postal workers won retention of the controversial no-layoff clause and a money package providing for a 14 per cent wage increase over two years. The contract also provided for four cost-of-living adjustments over the life of the contract, increasing base salary schedules one cent an hour for each 0.4-point increase in the Consumer Price Index.[30] This last provision actually ended up giving postal workers more of an increase than the guaranteed "up front" wage boost of $1100; the four cost-of-living adjustments during the 1973–1975 contract totaled $1,310.[31]

The 1973 agreement also included fringe benefit improvements that the letter carriers' union called a "significant breakthrough." [32] Whereas the Postal Service's share of the cost of employee life insurance previously had been about one third, the Service began paying 100 percent of the cost on July 20, 1974. Moreover, whereas the employer's share of health insurance premiums previously had been 40 per cent, the 1973 contract increased them to 55 per cent in July 1973, and to 65 per cent in July 1974.[33] Union leaders could not hide their pleasure over the favorable contract. The president of the powerful letter carriers' union told the members that he thought the contract was "in the dreamboat category." [34]

The 1975 Negotiations

By the third round of collective-bargaining talks, there was little doubt what the controversial points would be: the no-layoff clause, the up-front pay raise, the cost-of-living provisions, fringe benefits, management rights to dictate work rules, and overtime. The 1973 contract had proven very costly to the Postal Service, and management felt tremendous pressure to be tight-fisted. Thus, even when hundreds of East Coast postal workers staged protests at the Postal Service's Washington headquarters and at New York's main post office on 33rd Street in Manhattan, and even as talk of a postal strike quickened, management stood firm.[35] But the stalemate finally was broken on the last day of the contract, once again with the help of W. J. Usery, who called the settlement a victory for both parties and for collective bargaining. Though the unions won an increase to 75 per cent in the employer's share of health insurance premiums and managed to hold onto the no-layoff clause and the lucrative cost-of-living adjustments, the contract contained a relatively low wage increase of $1,500 in four installments over the life of the contract.[36]

The 1978 Negotiations

The fourth round of negotiations over a national contract came in 1978. The parties to the talks exhausted all the provisions of the Postal Reorganization Act and finally submitted to binding arbitration. The 1978 case thus merits greater elaboration because it reveals the full workings of the new collective bargaining and indicates the increasingly volatile atmosphere in which postal wage negotiations are conducted.

Once again all the important issues (no-layoff clause, cost-of-living adjustments, and the like) were on the bargaining table. But this time the controversies were set in a context even more politically charged than usual. The Postal Service had just come under the leadership of a new postmaster general, William F. Bolger, who succeeded Benjamin F. Bailar. Bolger had committed himself to a strenuous cost-cutting campaign. In addition, the Postal Service was under external pressures to hold down costs. The White House, as part of President Carter's inflation-control campaign, was publicly pressing postal management to stand firm and exercise restraint in the coming wage negotiations.[37]

As a further complicating factor, the two largest postal unions— the American Postal Workers Union (APWU) and the National Association of Letter Carriers (NALC)—faced closely contested presidential elections before the end of the year, and their leaders were under tremendous pressure from members (and from the challengers for their jobs) to improve on the 1975 contract. The president of the NALC, J. Joseph Vacca, was in his first term, and he lacked the substantial base of support given his predecessor, James H. Rademacher, who had led the union during the previous bargaining talks. In addition, Emmett Andrews had just succeeded the late Francis S. Filbey as president of the APWU, and had not yet faced an election of his own. The Postal Service worried about the effect these election races would have on the coming negotiations. As one Postal Service manager warned: "Those guys will be bargaining and running for election at the same time." [38] All these and other complicating factors contributed to making the 1978 negotiations particularly bitter and protracted.

Even before the talks began in April 1978, talk of a summer postal strike filled the air. Militant local union leaders in New York were predicting a walkout unless postal workers got higher pay raises and cost-of-living increases than those contained in the 1975 agreement.[39] In May the Postal Service responded to the increasing strike rhetoric by releasing a 49-page strike contingency plan, "Operation Graphic Hand." The plan revealed that in the event of a strike, the Postal Service was prepared to freeze pickup and delivery of most nonessential mail; take legal action against workers who might strike, picket, call in sick, or resign during the strike; set up special distribution centers to hand out or provide minimum delivery of the 71 million federal government checks that enter the mailstream each month; and provide special guarded air, train, and truck courier mail service from city to city.[40]

In June, four days before the unions were to make their first specific wage demands, the White House publicly called on the postal unions and management to reach a wage settlement in line with the administration's anti-inflation guidelines and urged Postal Service negotiators to be "as tough as they can" with the unions.[41] The White House intervention aggravated an already tense situation. The union presidents complained that the "irresponsible" White House efforts to "jawbone" them into holding wage demands around 5.5 percent were making it tougher for both sides to bargain.[42] Explaining that "no self-respecting union leader could possibly knuckle under to that kind of press-release interference with collective bargaining on the part of the White House," James LaPenta, a negotiator for the unions, said the Carter Administration's efforts would backfire: "What they're doing is self-defeating. They're being too public. Before, our members were mostly steamed up about rules, not wages. Now, they're all excited about wages, too." [43]

The wage demands presented by the unions on June 19th were for increases of $1,100 in the first year of a proposed two-year contract, and $865 in the next, along with a continuation of the automatic cost-of-living raises. These figures amounted to a 14 per cent wage increase in the first year, at least twice what the administration wanted the postal workers to accept.[44]

When management still had not responded by July 10, ten days before the expiration of the 1975 contract, federal mediators stepped into the negotiations. The talks continued while thousands of postal workers poured into Washington for massive demonstrations on July 12 to protest the slow progress of the bargaining and to strengthen the hands of the union negotiators.[45]

On July 15, management made its first wage offer (within the administration's 5.5 per cent limit for government workers), and the unions promptly rejected it. By this time it was clear that the principal stumbling block in the negotiations was the no-layoff clause. The Postal Service desperately wanted to get rid of the provision to reduce the workforce where feasible. The unions argued that the Postal Service already had cut 74,000 jobs through attrition since 1971, and that postal workers deserved job-security protections afforded other government workers. Both sides had taken rigid positions on the issue, and Wayne L. Horvitz, the chief federal mediator present at the negotiations, reported that the unions and management were "very far apart on everything." [46]

With the Postal Service and large mailers preparing for a postal strike as the final hours of the old contract waned, management suddenly broke the impasse in the talks by dropping its insistence on eliminating the no-layoff clause. Stopping the clock at midnight, the negotiators then turned to monetary issues and again became stuck. At the suggestion of Wayne Horvitz, Postmaster General William Bolger was summoned to the bargaining table at 2:30 A.M. He presented management's "final offer," and the unions accepted it. In terms of straight wage increases, the agreement called for 2 percent in the first year of the contract, 3 per cent in the second year, and 5 percent in the third year. The agreement also included six cost-of-living adjustments over the life of the contract but for the first time would put a limit, or "cap," on those adjustments.[47]

The tentative agreement was subject to ratification by union members in a mail balloting that would take several weeks. And although the national union leaders were not enthusiastic about the settlement, they expected it to be ratified. Some rank-and-file members and local union leaders, however, had a different view. Militant postal workers at the nation's largest bulk-mail-processing facility in Jersey City immediately walked off the job to protest the settlement, expressing dissatisfaction with the wage provisions and the capping of the cost-of-living adjustments.[48] Within a couple of days, workers at the huge San Francisco Bulk and Foreign Mail Center in Richmond, California, also walked off the job, calling the tentative contract a sellout and arguing that it allowed for excessive overtime scheduling and did not take into account the high cost of living in metropolitan areas. At raucous meetings in several other cities—Washington, Baltimore, Los Angeles, and Chicago—union members prepared to follow the lead of the Jersey City and San Francisco workers.[49]

The dissatisfaction with the proposed contract was fanned by Vincent Sombrotto, president of the huge Manhattan-Bronx branch of the NALC. Sombrotto, who was preparing to challenge NALC national president J. Joseph Vacca in the upcoming union election, announced: "I am absolutely dissatisfied with the way our leaders negotiated in Washington. It was a meaningless charade that they entered into with the Postmaster General and the White House." [50]

The next few weeks were filled with similar attacks against the national unions' leadership from Sombrotto and from Moe Biller, the president of the APWU's New York Metropolitan Area Chapter, which represents 23,000 workers, including many of the 4,500 at the Jersey City facility. Like Sombrotto, Biller had plans at some point to seek the presidency of the national union. (Both would win—Sombrotto in 1978, Biller in 1980—partly as a result of their militant posture, which appeals to many union members in the large cities.)

A wider strike was forestalled for the time being when Postmaster General Bolger, signaling his intention to deal firmly with those who might walk off the job, fired 80 strikers in Jersey City and 42 in San Francisco and announced his intention to "do the same wherever this happens." [51]

But by the last week in August, the prospects of a nationwide postal strike again appeared strong as the results of the union membership ratification votes were tabulated. The NALC members rejected the tentative contract by a 72,288 to 58,832 vote. The letter carriers' union was the first to vote, and it was bound by its constitution to strike if bargaining did not resume within five days, even though postal strikes are illegal under federal law. Vacca, caught between the conflicting requirements of the law and of his union's constitution, called on Postmaster General William Bolger to reopen contract talks. Bolger had earlier insisted that the Postal Service absolutely would not resume negotiations, since the law provided a clearly defined procedure for such situations—fact-finding and binding arbitration.[52]

The likelihood of a postal strike seemed to increase still further when, two days later, the rank-and-file members of two more unions joined the letter carriers in rejecting the proposed contract. The APWU voted 94,400 to 78,487 against the contract—roughly the same margin by which the letter carriers had earlier turned down the pact. The mail handlers also rejected the settlement. The APWU vote elicited a statement from Postmaster General Bolger, who described the situation as serious but gave no indication that the Postal Service would meet union demands for a new round of bargaining, even though the Federal Mediation and Conciliation Service was urging the Postal Service to abandon its no-bargaining stance.[53]

As the strike deadline approached, the leaders of the NALC and the APWU faced a no-win predicament: defy the law and risk jail and fines for the unions, or defy official directives of their own unions and risk internal political reprisals.

The nation was once again girding for a postal strike, when with fewer than eight hours to go before another midnight strike deadline, the Postal Service and union leaders agreed to a compromise procedure (permitted under the terms of the reorganization act) for resolving their contract dispute. The agreement, drawn by the chief federal mediator, Wayne Horvitz, combined the unions' demand for more negotiations and management's call for arbitration. The agreement provided for a resumption of bargaining followed by binding arbitration if the two sides failed to reach a settlement within fifteen days.[54]

The Federal Mediation and Conciliation Service selected James J. Healy, a professor of industrial relations at the Harvard Business School, to mediate the talks between the Postal Service and the unions. But during the fifteen-day discussions, Healy was unable to secure a resolution of the disputes between the two parties, so on September 15, 1978, he imposed a binding settlement. The arbitrator gave postal workers a salary increase slightly larger than the one contained in the rejected contract. More important, Healy removed the cap that had been put on the cost-of-living raises. Whereas the rejected pact would have limited the total cost-of-living increase over the three-year life of the contract to 73 cents an hour (roughly $1,300), the arbitrated settlement permitted six semiannual increases based on a 1-cent raise for each full 0.4-point increase in the Consumer Price Index.[55] (The effect of this decision has been great, providing postal workers once again with a larger pay increase under the cost-of-living provision than under the up-front wage boost. By December 1980, with one more increase yet to come under the 1978 contract, the cost-of-living raises had increased the average postal worker's salary almost $3,000 annually.)[56]

But in spite of these increases in the proposed contract's wage provisions, Healy granted postal management little in exchange. The Postal Service had been hoping Healy would eliminate the no-layoff provision. But instead of eliminating or watering down the job-protection language, Healy strengthened it for workers already employed by the Postal Service as of September 15, 1978, ordering that they should be guarded from layoffs for their "work lifetime" rather than just for the lifetime of each contract. They can, of course, still be fired for gross incompetence or for crimes committed while on duty, but they cannot be laid off because of automation or the like. However, new workers (anyone hired after September 15, 1978) have to work six years before they earn lifetime job protection.

Perspectives on Postal Collective Bargaining

From the preceding account, it should be clear that postal workers have done well under the new arrangements for setting wages and benefits. The postal unions are not reluctant to point to the gains their members have made as a result of the advent of collective bargaining. One union leader has proudly claimed: "The fact is that we have gained substantially larger raises across the board in negotiations with postal management than we ever did politicking on Capitol Hill." [57]

Indeed, postal workers have come to a position where they enjoy (as one union official put it) "the best of both worlds," the private and the public sectors. Postal workers have the right to bargain with their employer over wages, benefits, and working conditions.

They also have the power that comes from being able to reinforce bargaining demands with plausible strike threats. Moreover, the postal unions continue to find respectful attention on Capitol Hill, where their formidable organizational and financial strength, combined with skill at the "art of lobbying," accords them an unusually prominent role. The postal unions continue to appear before congressional committees regularly. They may be working, for example, to secure improved civil service retirement benefits, which postal workers continue to receive even though they are no longer part of the regular civil service. The unions also have substantial influence in shaping postal policy decisions that are essentially managerial—for example, whether to move from six-day to five-day delivery or whether to continue the Postal Service's legal monopoly on the delivery of first-class letters.

Taking politics out of postal wage-setting (that is, ending congressional and presidential responsibility for establishing postal wages) was supposed to accomplish two objectives: (1) to give postal management a more direct part in determining the compensation levels of postal workers; and (2) to enable postal management to control labor costs and reduce the percentage of the system's total costs accounted for by employee wages and benefits.

This second objective was the more problematical, for its implicit assumption was that management would be better able to stand firm before union wage demands than the elected officials would, since they had in their electoral constituencies the legions of geographically dispersed and well-organized postal workers. But the cases presented above suggest that postal management is not really in a much better position to hold the line on wage demands. Several factors, in addition to the general pressures of high inflation, account for this outcome.

First, unlike unionized workers in private-sector industries who have to show some restraint in their wage demands lest they force their employer out of business, postal workers have no such incentive to exercise restraint. They know that even if their higher wages cause growing deficits, that will not spell the collapse of the Postal Service. They know (or surmise) that the postal system would be maintained, if necessary, by recourse to the public treasury.

A second, similar source of inflationary pressure on postal wages is the Postal Service's legal monopoly on delivering letter mail. The postal unions vigorously support continuation of the monopoly because they assume that as long as it keeps the demand for letter-delivery service reasonably inelastic, they can push wages up without driving all the business away. The Postal Service's letter-mail monopoly, in effect, confers a monopoly on the unions.

Third, the Postal Service is reluctant to stand too firmly in the face of union strike threats because executives fear that a massive postal strike would be a blow from which the Postal Service might never fully recover. Users of second-, third-, and fourth-class mail would be driven to find alternative delivery systems from which the Postal Service might be unable to recapture them. Moreover, the Postal Service has (so far) been under pressure from those same mailers, and also from the general public and political elites, to avoid a strike because of the potential crippling effect on the economy and because of the general inconvenience it would cause those who depend on the mail system.

Whatever the defects of the pre-reorganization method of setting postal wages, the system had its virtues. The presence of third-party decision makers (Congress, the President, and the Bureau of the Budget) tempered relations between management and the rank-and-file employees. Now, however, the unions and management face each other across the bargaining table without the luxury of intermediaries on whom responsibility devolves. Whereas before the reorganization both parties saw themselves as constituent parts of the same service agency, they now see themselves more as independent adversaries. This development obviously makes it difficult to achieve consensus throughout the Postal Service about the organization's current practices or future policies. It is not uncommon for government agencies to adopt an "us versus them" outlook toward Congress and the White House or toward various external clientele groups; in the Postal Service, however, this adversary relation has been institutionalized inside the organization by the advent of collective bargaining.

The difference in attitude is most pronounced with the unions, whose members' principal attachments have changed. They now are union members first and postal workers second. This change followed from the maturation of the postal unions after the postal reorganization and shows in the increased union strength and militancy, partly an outcome of the 1970 mergers. The unions have adopted a more aggressive posture now. Some of this stems from the increasing militancy of public employee unions in general throughout the late 1960s and 1970s. Strikes by municipal workers are now commonplace. This development has encouraged the postal unions to use demonstrations and strike threats to back their demands for improved wages and benefits. Strikes by other public workers have helped to make the postal unions' strike threats more potent by showing that it is not the legal right to strike that counts, but the will and the ability to do so.

The postal unions' increased militancy is also the result of pressure exerted on national union leaders by the heads of militant local unions, especially in New York City. For years Vincent Sombrotto and Morris Biller pushed the unions toward more aggressive stances. But now Sombrotto and Biller have won the national presidencies of their unions—the NALC and the APWU, respectively—and are sure to draw a hard line in contract negotiations. Whatever happens in future talks, relations between postal labor and management are likely to become even more strained in the next few years, especially if the Reagan Administration and Congress push the Postal Service to find additional ways to cut spending.

In sum, there have been radical alterations in the institutions and procedures for setting postal wages. These changes have had some important consequences for the distribution of political power in the postal policy arena and have unintentionally inflated postal costs. These costs must be recovered by rate increases. And as we shall now see, important changes have also occurred in the process and politics of setting postal rates.

Endnotes

1. Michael L. Brookshire and Michael L. Rogers, *Collective Bargaining in the Public Sector* (Lexington, Mass.: Lexington Books, 1977), p. 2.
2. Sterling D. Spero, *The Labor Movement in a Government Industry* (New York: George H. Doran Co., 1924), p. 57.
3. *Ibid.*, p. 58.
4. *Ibid.*, p. 61.
5. *Ibid.*, chap. 6, and pp. 103–104, 300–303.
6. Quoted in *ibid.*, pp. 85–86.
7. Quoted in *ibid.*, p. 97.
8. Sterling D. Spero, *Government as Employer* (Carbondale: Southern Illinois Press, 1948), chap. 8.
9. President's Commission on Postal Organization, Report of the Commission,

Towards Postal Excellence (Washington: U.S. Government Printing Office, 1968), Annex, vol. 4, part 7, p. 44.

10. *Washington Post*, July 23, 1967, p. A22; cited in Richard F. Fenno, Jr., *Congressmen in Committees* (Boston: Little, Brown, 1973), p. 37.
11. William C. Doherty, *Mailman U.S.A.* (New York: David McKay and Co., 1960), pp. 21–22, 189. Doherty was for many years the president of the National Association of Letter Carriers.
12. For a description of the postal unions' lobbying activities, see Fenno, *Congressmen in Committees*, pp. 41–42, 242–255.
13. *Ibid.*, pp. 64, 66.
14. *Ibid.*, p. 246.
15. Quoted in *ibid.*, p. 247.
16. *Ibid.*, p. 246.
17. *Union Postal Clerk* (April 1971), pp. 2–4.
18. *Union Postal Clerk* (June 1971), pp. 2–3.
19. Spero, *Labor Movement*, pp. 79–80.
20. *Ibid.*
21. James H. Rademacher, in *The Postal Record* (April 1971), pp. 4–5. *The Postal Record* is the monthly magazine of the National Association of Letter Carriers.
22. *Union Postal Clerk* (May 1971), p. 4.
23. *Ibid.*, pp. 4, 5.
24. "Report to the Parties by Fact-Finding Panel in Re the Dispute between Seven National Postal Unions and the United States Post Office Department," June 7, 1971.
25. Summary of July 20, 1971, labor agreement, mimeographed, undated, pp. 1–6.
26. *Postal Record* (August 1974), p. 10.
27. *Ibid.*
28. *Ibid.*, p. 11.
29. *Ibid.*
30. United States Postal Service, *Working Agreement*, July 20, 1971, Article 21, Sections 1–4.
31. *Washington Post*, August 23, 1975, p. D2.
32. National Association of Letter Carriers, *Bulletin*, no. 15, July 2, 1973.
33. United States Postal Service, *National Agreement*, July 21, 1973, Article 21.
34. *Postal Record* (August 1974), p. 11.
35. For accounts of the demonstrations, see *New York Times*, June 18, 1975, p. 19; July 8, 1975, p. 27.
36. United States Postal Service, *National Agreement*, July 21, 1975, Articles 6, 9, and 21.
37. *New York Times*, April 19, 1978, p. 15.
38. *Ibid.*
39. *Washington Post*, March 22, 1978, p. E2.
40. *Washington Post*, May 17, 1978, p. D2.
41. *New York Times*, June 19, 1978, p. 16.
42. *Washington Post*, June 14, 1978, p. C2.
43. *New York Times*, June 19, 1978, p. 16.

44. *Washington Post,* June 20, 1978, p. 1.
45. *New York Times,* July 13, 1978, p. A17; and *Washington Post,* July 13, 1978, p. A3.
46. *New York Times,* July 15, 1978, p. 43.
47. *New York Times,* July 22, 1978, pp. 1, 8.
48. *Ibid.,* p. 8.
49. *New York Times,* July 24, 1978, p. 1.
50. *New York Times,* July 22, 1978, p. 8.
51. *Associated Press,* July 25, 1978.
52. *Washington Post,* August 24, 1978, p. A1.
53. *Washington Post,* August 26, 1978, p. A1.
54. *Washington Post,* August 29, 1978, p. A1. The Postal Reorganization Act provided that labor and management may devise a procedure of their own choosing for a binding resolution of their differences. (*United States Code,* Title 39, sec. 1207).
55. *Washington Post,* September 16, 1978, pp. A1, A3.
56. On effects of uncapping the cost-of-living adjustment provision, see *Postal Record* (May 1980), pp. 4, 5; and also see *Washington Post,* November 11, 1980, p. C2.
57. American Postal Workers Union, *American Postal Worker* (October 1973), p. 10.

Chapter 5

SETTING RATES: CHANGES IN INSTITUTIONS AND PROCESSES

Save for the change in the organization's seal (the colonial rider gave way to an eagle poised for flight), nothing about the reconstituted Postal Service could be more noticeable to users of the mail system than the sharp increase in the rates charged for mail services. Between 1971 and 1978, increases in postage rates on four different occasions raised the price of a first-class stamp by 150 per cent, from 6 cents to 15 cents. Sharp increases of this kind in recent years for all mail classes (and much higher *percentage* increases in second class, for example) are the consequence of two factors. These are the Service's higher revenue requirements, pushed up by soaring costs, and the provision in the Postal Reorganization Act requiring that operating revenue equal, "as nearly as practicable," the system's total costs—in other words, that the Postal Service try to break even.

Less obvious to mail users, but at least as important, are the changes during this period in the way postal rates are set. The 1968 President's Commission on Postal Organization had concluded that the political pressures inherent in legislative rate-making had resulted in a complex, irrational rate structure that had no reasonable connection to the postal system's revenue requirements or to the costs of providing specific services.[1] The changes that have since

103

occurred in the institutions and procedures for setting postal rates have been profound and have had important consequences.

Setting Rates before the Reorganization

In the two decades before the postal reorganization, postal rate policies grew in political importance. New programs in other fields were placing heavy demands on the federal budget. The financial condition of the postal enterprise itself was worsening. And the presence of many large mailing industries with special interests and demands made postal rates and classifications genuine political issues; different groups and individuals fought for government subsidization of their specific interests.

Control over the process of revising the postal rate structure rested not with the Post Office Department itself but with Congress and the Bureau of the Budget (BOB). In fact, it was not uncommon in those years for the initial impetus for a rate increase to come from the budget examiners in BOB assigned to monitor the financial condition of the Post Office. If the BOB and the White House decided that a rate adjustment was fiscally necessary and politically feasible, the Office of Postal Economics in the Post Office Department would be called on to produce initial drafts of a revised rate structure and justifications therefor.[2]

Postal and budget officials normally took informal soundings with key congressmen during the drafting stages of a rate bill to discover what rates the legislators considered politically possible. The department also sought reactions from the heavy users of specific classes of mail—magazine publishers, direct-mail advertisers, mail-order companies, and the like. For example, after the Office of Postal Economics had completed the staff paper on possible rate proposals in anticipation of the 1967 rate bill, postal officials held discussions on an informal, off-the-record basis with numerous large mailers. About twenty to thirty different groups and associations were informed of the planned rate increases, and their comments were taken as a measure of "what the traffic would bear." [3]

The Post Office Department and the BOB, working within the limits defined by these early consultations, would then formulate a legislative proposal by, in effect, taking its estimate of what the traffic (and Congress) would bear and adding 10 per cent for bargaining purposes. A rate hike proposal, once drafted, had to await a politically propitious time for submission to Congress, even if delay meant still higher postal deficits. In what finally became the 1968 rate increase, for example, it was clear to the BOB and the Post Office as early as 1964 that an overall rate increase was required. But because of concerns over the effect an increase would have on congressmen's electoral fortunes in the 1966 elections, rate legislation was not submitted until April 1967, postponed three years from when the need was first recognized.[4]

The dominance of political expediency over economic considerations in pre-reorganization postal rate-making was even more apparent once a rate measure had been submitted to Congress and was under deliberation. Congressional hearings on a rate bill (usually held first before the Subcommittee on Postal Rates of the House Committee on Post Office and Civil Service) provided a public forum in which the Post Office and organized mail users could give their views to elected officials. During the opening few days of hearings, Post Office Department officials would present the administration's case for the rate increases, typically emphasizing the severity of the agency's financial situation, while also taking care to show that the agency's rate request was based on an appreciation of the political constraints on the legislators. At a House hearing in 1967, for example, Assistant Postmaster General Ralph Nicholson explained why the Post Office Department had not requested much higher second-class rates:[5]

> *In 1962, the Department did propose a sharp increase in second-class rates. After various consideration both in the House and in the Senate, the Congress ultimately enacted rate increases that were substantially less than those that we proposed. We feel that the ones we have recommended this time are similar to those that were processed by the Congress after many weeks of careful consideration, hearing all sides of the story. And it is in that spirit we have brought you again a proposal that seems to reflect the intent of Congress. That is the kind of rate increase that you would find desirable, practical, and in the public interest.*

After testimony from administration representatives, a parade of organized mail users—publishers, church groups, greeting-card manufacturers, sound-recording producers—would argue for leaving the rates undisturbed or reducing the increases requested by the administration. In their presentations, the mailing interests sought to persuade committee members that widespread distribution of their products was in the public interest, and that the proposed rate changes would impose on them an undue share of the total adjusted rate burden, having a devastatingly adverse effect on their operations. The hearings were filled with visions of magazines having to cease publication, direct-mail advertising companies going bankrupt, and the nation's intellectual and commercial exchange breaking down.[6] (The intensity with which some mailers made such assertions was in no way diminished by the absence of firm evidence to support the claims.)

After the hearings, the subcommittee would go into executive session to review them and mark up the bill, a process that frequently caused dramatic changes in the proposal. During consideration of the 1967 rate bill, for example, the House subcommittee substantially altered all 27 points in the measure.[7] Rate bills were open to still further amendment after submission to the full committee and again after debate began on the House floor. Through these stages, the initial form of the legislation as introduced by the executive branch usually changed considerably when the legislators sought to accommodate the wishes of various mailing industries. The main changes usually came in the committee; its members dealt with the intense pressure from the mailers' organizations by adopting as their decision rule on rate bills, "oppose all rate increases for mail users." [8]

If Senate hearings were held, the arguments presented there tended to duplicate those presented during the House hearings. Senate deliberations and, if necessary, conference committee reconciliations, provided further opportunities for changes in the rate proposals.

Several features of this extended legislative process worked to the relative advantage of organized mail users. First, the process was highly permeable, affording interested organizations many opportunities to shape the course of rate legislation. Indeed, the process may have been *too* permeable, as suggested by several bribery scandals that occurred in the 1960s; direct mailers were held to be buying the votes of influential members of the post office committees.[9]

Second, legislative rate-making did not rely heavily on rigorous examination of the economic implications of rate issues. That is, congressional hearings were characterized less by sophisticated economic presentations, careful cross-examinations, and rebuttals than by relatively simple and repetitive expressions of self-interest on the part of organized special mailers. This pattern saved mail users the expense of preparing rigorous, carefully documented arguments.

Finally, time was on the side of the interest groups. The legislative process provided them with both the opportunity and the incentive to prolong the proceedings, the objective being to delay enactment; each day that passed without higher rates represented a "savings" to the mailers. During the lengthy proceedings surrounding the 1967 rate bill, for example, each week's delay meant the loss of close to $15 million in expected federal revenue, and that much saved by the mailers collectively.[10]

Drawbacks to Legislative Rate-Making

As the economic issues of setting postal rates became more complex, and as the political atmosphere surrounding rate formulation grew increasingly volatile, legislative rate-making came to be widely regarded as inadequate for the task at hand. Its many deficiencies seemed all too apparent to the postal reformers. First, because of the magnitude, in both volume and importance, of other matters on the congressional agenda, the postal rate schedule received low legislative priority. There simply were too many other matters increasingly attracting the attention and demanding the time of legislators. Rate bills were routinely delayed for months, even years.

Second, the congressional subcommittees were not particularly well equipped to deal with the complex economic and regulatory issues raised by the rate bills. The multiple and conflicting duties of legislators denied committee members an opportunity to learn about the intricacies of postal rate matters. This problem was aggravated by the relatively rapid turnover of membership on postal subcommittees, caused at least partly by the low prestige attached to such committee assignments.[11] Very few members of either the House or the Senate postal committees had been members for ten years. In 1967 the House Post Office and Civil Service Committee had 26 members. Three (all Republicans) had been on the committee for a decade. In the Senate, the 12-member committee had 2 members (1 Democrat, 1 Republican) who had been on the committee since 1957. Indeed, most had a tenure of only about three years, hardly enough time to develop much technical expertise in regulating rates; thus it was even more likely that rate issues would be considered on political rather than on economic grounds. Moreover, the committee staff members were not even in a position to pick up the slack here. Although the staff support was reportedly competent, it was (in the view of consultants to the 1968 President's Commission on Postal Organization) "too limited to do proper justice to the task." [12]

Third, this lack of expertise in setting rates, combined with the time constraints, forced the committees to deal with rate issues in a relatively perfunctory manner. In the usual hearing format, a legion of interested organizations would parade before the committees to present their views and respond to superficial questions or comments from committee members. The hearings were dominated by the mailers' pleadings for congressional restraint in raising rates and by the legislators' attempts to show their heartfelt concern for the problems of the politically powerful mailers. [13]

Thus, postal reformers sought an alternative to congressional rate-making because of its obvious inadequacies and its highly politicized character. Indeed, one of the chief purposes of the whole postal reorganization was to take politics out of setting postal rates. By *politics* postal reformers meant generally the efforts of organized mailers to persuade elected officials to accommodate their demands in the design of a rate schedule. To postal reformers, the irrationality of the rate structure and the poor financial health of the postal enterprise were adequate evidence that the special mailers were achieving their objectives. The continuation of this old process of setting postal rates would surely stand in the way of what postal reformers considered essential for the mail system's fiscal health— the design of a more economically rational rate structure, one more realistically connected to the actual costs of operating the system.

The reformers found their solution in the standard model for public utility regulation. The Post Office, after all, was an anachronism. It was the only public service of national importance for which the legislature had retained the prerogative for setting rates. The rates for natural gas, electricity, telephone, and transportation services all were being regulated by full-time commissions that, with the aid of technically trained staffs, approved rates after reviewing extensive accounting and engineering data and economic evidence. These commissions based rate decisions on the record of evidentiary proceedings in which due process safeguards were carefully observed. Postal reformers wanted postal rates set under similar arrangements.[14]

Although architects of the postal reorganization appreciated the differences between postal service and the services rendered by traditional public utilities, the differences, they argued, were primarily in form. And though postal reformers recognized that other factors besides cost and economic efficiency were properly to be considered in establishing rates and fees for postal services, they concluded that "economic science does provide standards for postal rate-making"; and they urged, therefore, that procedures and economic principles observed in the operation and regulation of other economic enterprises should be applied to postal service also.[15]

Setting Rates after the Reorganization

The Postal Reorganization Act took postal rate-making away from Congress and established all new procedures and institutional machinery for setting rates. Postal Service rate increases must now be reviewed by the Postal Rate Commission (PRC), an independent regulatory agency established in 1971 to consider Postal Service requests for changing rates, mail classifications, and services. The commission has five members appointed by the President, confirmed by the Senate, and assisted by a trained staff of accountants, economists, and lawyers; and it holds formal, quasi-judicial hearings at which interested parties have the opportunity to present arguments and data and to cross-examine witnesses for the Postal Service and the other intervenors.

Once the PRC has made its determinations, it issues a "recommended decision" to the Postal Service board of governors. The board may approve the recommendation and order the rates to be put in effect, or it may completely reject the proposal and start all over. The governors are also free to reject the PRC's recommended decision and resubmit the rate request to the commission for its reconsideration. When the PRC then renders a new decision, the governors can modify the decision by a unanimous vote.[16] As the following analysis of these new processes shows, the changes have largely achieved the intent of postal reformers, substantially removing rate matters from the domain of elected officials and injecting the postal rate-making process with more professionalism.

Following the postal reorganization, the Postal Service has had independent responsibility for developing accurate data about the costs of its services and for making sure that its proposed rates, based on those data, will generate sufficient revenues to allow the Postal Service to break even. Thus, when postal executives determine that changes in rates and fees are necessary, the Postal Service prepares a formal rate request to be submitted to the rate commission. This alone is an important change from the old procedure. It means that decisions to go ahead with a change in postage rates are now based solely on the Postal Service's revenue needs, and that the decision to seek an increase is no longer constrained or delayed by congressional or presidential concerns about the electoral costs of such a move.

The Postal Service rate requests consist of volumes of information and data explaining the nature, scope, significance, and effect of the proposed rate and fee changes. The most important parts of the request are the data explaining the attribution and assignment of costs to specific services or classes of mail and the design of rates based on those costing data. (All this is treated in detail in the next chapter.)

When the Postal Rate Commission receives a request from the Postal Service for a recommended decision on a rate increase, the commission schedules evidentiary hearings and may appoint a hearing examiner (usually a senior lawyer on the staff who is experienced in rate issues); the examiner acts as a judge at the hearings.[17] The examiner issues a notice of prehearing conference at which the issues are defined and simplified, positions are presented by parties to the case, and agreement is reached on the various exhibits that will constitute the evidence to be presented at the hearings.

It is at the hearing and deliberation stage that the new procedures stand in the sharpest contrast to practices under legislative rate-making. The hearings themselves are a lengthy set of formal fact-finding arguments before the commissioners (or before the hearing examiner if the commissioners have chosen not to hear the cases themselves, as in the first two rate cases). The entire hearing procedure is very formal and bound by strict rules. Parties are free to file briefs, make oral arguments, and offer witnesses of their own, subject to cross-examination by all other intervenors. All this can make for an extraordinarily complicated case when the intervenors number as high as sixty, including all the main mailing industry trade associations, such as the Magazine Publishers Association, the Direct Mail Marketing Association, the American Newspaper Publishers Association, and the American Bankers Association. Attorneys for the Postal Service and for each of the intervenors develop as strong a case as possible in support of their position. And as the official record in a case is being built, the commission is responsible for ensuring that a complete and ordered body of facts is developed, from which a decision can be reached. At the conclusion of the hearings, the examiner (or the commissioner acting as presiding officer) fixes dates for filing briefs; these documents may include proposed findings of fact, conclusions of law, or references to specific parts of the record and supporting expert testimony or exhibits.[18]

When this whole process is over, the commission has before it the monumental task of analyzing the entire record—the examiner's initial decision (if there is one), the various filings, testimony of experts, interrogatories and answers, exhibits, briefs and replies, and oral arguments. The commission, in evaluating all this information (13,000 pages' worth in the first rate case), is required to take into account the following criteria set down by Congress in the Postal Reorganization Act:[19]

1. *The establishment and maintenance of a fair and equitable schedule.*
2. *The value of the mail service actually provided each class or type of mail service to both the sender and the recipient, including but not limited to the collection, mode of transportation, and priority of delivery.*
3. *The requirement that each class of mail or type of mail service bear the direct and indirect postal costs attributable to that class or type plus that portion of all other costs of the Postal Service reasonably assignable to such class or type.*
4. *The effect of rate increases upon the general public, business mail users, and enterprises in the private sector of the economy engaged in the delivery of mail matter other than letters.*
5. *The available alternative means of sending and receiving letters and other mail matter at reasonable costs.*
6. *The degree of preparation of mail for delivery into the postal system performed by the mailer and its effect upon reducing costs to the Postal Service.*
7. *Simplicity of structure for the entire schedule and simple, identifiable relationships between the rates or fees charged the various classes of mail for postal services.*
8. *Such other factors as the Commission deems appropriate.*

When the commission has finally reached a decision, the supporting evidence and governing legal and policy principles are detailed in an extensive document issued as a recommended decision by the commission to the Postal Service board of governors.

The contrast between this process and the legislative rate-making detailed earlier is striking. Perhaps the most obvious difference is in the relations among the Postal Service, the organized mail users, and the rate reviewers (previously Congress, now the rate commission). Before the reorganization, the hearings and other proceedings were handled in a highly informal, hail-fellow atmosphere in which political maneuvering was the rule. Postal reformers had worried that this process made it too easy for the special interests to exercise untoward influence over postal rates. The new process with its formal, depoliticized, legalistic, adversary hearings, is designed to inject more rigor and professionalism into setting postal rates. Whatever effect these changes may have had on the elegance or economic rationality of postal rate-making (a subject to be explored in the next chapter), the new procedures have undeniably altered the rules of the game, changed the set of players, and raised the stakes.

Since postal reformers attached special importance to procedural fairness in the new process, they wanted to provide special safeguards for isolating the commissioners and staff members of the PRC from pressure by organized mail users. Thus, after Congress passed the Postal Reorganization Act in 1970, two members of the House Post Office and Civil Service Committee, Representatives Morris K. Udall (Dem., Ariz.) and David N. Henderson (Dem., N.C.), wrote to President Richard Nixon urging him to develop appropriate standards of conduct for the rate commissioners and their staff and to choose carefully when selecting commissioners. The congressmen expressed concern that "one of the potential dangers of the new arrangement is that the intensive, well-financed and expert lobbying activities previously directed to Congress will be primarily focused on the five members of the commission." [20]

As a result of these urgings, President Nixon issued Executive Order 11570, directing the Civil Service Commission to prepare standards of conduct for the new rate commission. [21] When the Civil Service Commission issued its regulations on March 23, 1971, it explained that the rules were stringent because the personal conduct of commission personnel "must at all times be unquestionably free from taint or suspicion of impartiality, favoritism, or any indicia of conflicting interests." [22]

Among the most important rules is the one governing *ex parte* communications, prohibiting employees of the commission, and the commissioners themselves, from engaging in one-sided discussions regarding either a substantive or a procedural matter that is at issue or that may become an issue before the commission.[23] The rule, common among regulatory agencies, requires the commission to solicit rebuttal information from all interested parties if it accepts information from any interested party.

The elaborate set of rules included other standards also designed to shield the agency's officers from outside pressures. The rules of conduct tightly restrict commissioners and employees in their financial holdings in any entity that may be significantly affected by rates, fees, or classifications of mail. Soliciting or accepting gifts, favors, entertainment, and the like from parties having or wanting business with the Postal Service is forbidden. The rules even direct each employee to pay personal bills "in a proper and timely manner," which is defined to mean, "in a manner which the commission determines does not, under the circumstances, reflect adversely on the commission as his employer." [24] These and other provisions are intended to increase the likelihood of integrity and independence in regulating postal rates.

The only incident marring the PRC's otherwise unsullied reputation centered on an alleged conflict of interest involving A. Lee Fritschler, a chairman of the PRC, who bought a $75,900 vacation apartment with Joel Yahalem, his friend of fifteen years and general solicitor for Western Union. The conflict-of-interest flap arose over Fritschler's participation in a case before the PRC relating to an agreement between the Postal Service and Western Union to operate a joint, low-priced electronic message service. But there is no reason to suspect that there was a genuine conflict of interest here, and no evidence exists to suggest that the PRC's conduct standards are not having their intended effect.[25]

Besides all these changes in the rules governing setting rates, other important changes have occurred in the cast of persons involved. Economists and cost analysts are now especially prominent in the revised proceedings. The formal evidentiary hearings have forced the special mailers to assemble much better evidence in support of their cases than they did for the legislative hearings, in which the presentations tended to be emotionally and politically appealing but poorly substantiated. In the new adversary proceedings, each party strives for every possible advantage and tries to expose weaknesses in opponents' arguments; intervenors must now, therefore, have good enough data to make credible arguments, and to be successful, must have evidence that can withstand all-round close scrutiny. Consequently, mailers' associations have had to hire professional economists and cost analysts to bolster their arguments and to dissect the presentations of other intervenors. The huge Direct Mail/Marketing Association (DMMA), for example, employs Arthur Eden, who used to be assistant postmaster general for rates and classifications at the Postal Service. The DMMA and other mailers' associations rely on the experts to help them construct defensible arguments about the correctness of the Postal Service's cost attributions and assignments.[26]

Although economists and costing and rate experts are newly prominent in the procedure for setting postal rates, it is the lawyer's role that has been most enhanced by the changes. The legal formalities, after all, are even more tangled and complex than the economic issues. Since evidentiary hearings are very strict on procedure, an intervenor's chances of successful participation rest on the shoulders of counsel who can maneuver through the labyrinth of legal notices, pleadings, interrogatories, examination and cross-examination, and findings. So important is expert legal assistance in this process that the large mailers' associations spare no expense in retaining the best legal help they can find. The DMMA, for example, hires partners from the prestigious Washington law firm, Covington and Burling.[27]

The new reliance on economists and lawyers underlines the whole change in setting rates. One veteran third-class mail lobbyist has described the difference between legislative and regulatory rate-making this way:[28]

> *You have to document everything. It's the difference between sandlot baseball and the big leagues. . . . The way it used to be done is no longer acceptable. . . . Everything we do now is reviewed by economists and lawyers, ten times more than ever before. Every single word we use becomes important.*

All these changes have had two important effects, both of which have left the mailers' organizations in a relatively weakened position. First, the new rate-review process has dramatically increased the costs incurred by mail users' associations for their participation in rate proceedings. One estimate is that an intervenor must spend a quarter of a million dollars a year to present the kind of detailed analysis that will have any effect on the proceedings.[29] The DMMA, for example, claims that the changes have doubled that organization's expenses, largely because of the use of outside consultants and lawyers, as well as the extra time spent by the organization's own staff members.[30] These soaring costs of participation in the postal rate proceedings preclude the involvement of mail users' groups or interested individual mailers anxious to press their case but lacking substantial financial resources.

A second important effect of the professionalization of postal rate-making is the tremendously enhanced importance of *information* as a resource. Rate cases now center on careful analysis of extensive data about postal revenue requirements, cost attributions, demand elasticities, economic effects on large mailers, and the like. Though mail users and competitive delivery systems are investing huge sums of money in acquiring their own information and expertise, they still find themselves at a disadvantage in facing the relatively information-rich Postal Service. A complaint during the second rate case from the National Association of Greeting Card Publishers is typical: "None of us private parties have the opportunity to get into the statistical detail that the Postal Service has. We're operating at a disadvantage." [31]

Not only are the intervenors' own information sources not as extensive as those of the Postal Service, but these organizations actually depend on the Postal Service for much of their information, such as volume estimates. Thus, the Postal Service is in a superior position as a result of its control over scarce information resources. Though the Postal Service is supposed to honor requests from rate-case participants for information, it can effectively refrain from doing so merely by dragging its feet or claiming not to have the data. Even the Postal Rate Commission depends somewhat on the Postal Service's informational beneficence, as a former rate commissioner explained to a congressional committee:[32]

> . . . *With relatively few exceptions they gave us everything they could. And that is always hard to judge, because they are sitting on the data, and when you ask for something, and they say, "Jiminy, it's*

*awful hard to get this," or that it will cost a certain number of dollars,
you have to take their word for it.*

The problem, as Clyde S. DuPont (another former PRC chairman)
says, is that the PRC lacks[33]

*explicit statutory authority . . . to prescribe or require the Postal
Service to collect particular types of data. Although our discovery
powers are generally sufficient to permit us to test and clarify evidence presented in our proceedings, the service has treated the actual
collection of data as its exclusive domain. It reserves the design of its
statistical systems and the data to be released as a matter of unilateral
discretion. . . . Thus, the commission and the parties to our proceedings have been tied to the data the Postal Service is willing and able to
make available.*

In sum, the reorganization succeeded in removing the setting of
postal rates from the legislative arena, where organized mail users
exercised their political influence to persuade legislators that the
low-cost distribution of their material (magazines, newspapers,
books, records, greeting cards, advertising, and the like) was in the
public interest. Under the new arrangement, the congressional role
is largely eliminated, and technical arguments over cost attribution
and assignment tend to dominate the formal proceedings. Information and substantive expertise are now at a premium. All this has
profoundly affected the role of the various mailing interests in making the rates.

In spite of all this, however, the basic structure of postal rates—
the rough share of the total cost burden shouldered by the various
classes of mail users—has changed astonishingly little; first-class
mail users continue to pay more than their share of the system's
total costs. Let us now examine why this is so—why a matter as
seemingly prosaic as allocating postal costs can provoke bitter political controversy.

Endnotes

1. President's Commission on Postal Organization, Report of the Commission,
   Towards Postal Excellence (Washington: U.S. Government Printing Office,
   1968), p. 146.
2. *Ibid.*, Annex, vol. 2, "Rates and Rate-Making," p. 8-2.
3. Arthur D. Little, Inc., "Procedural Matters Related to Establishing Postal
   Classifications and Setting Postal Rates," Working Memorandum FLA/CM-3,

September 1967, p. 5. This "working memorandum" was one of a series prepared by consultants to the President's Commission on Postal Organization.

4. *Ibid.*, pp. 18, 21.

5. U.S., Congress, House, Committee on Post Office and Civil Service, *The Postal Revenue Act of 1967, Hearings on H.R. 7977 and H.R. 7978, before a subcommittee of the Committee on Post Office and Civil Service*, 90th Cong., 1st Sess., 1967, p. 60.

6. *Ibid.* See, for example, pp. 152–153, 541–548.

7. For a good account of the compromises and amendments, see *Congressional Quarterly Almanac*, vol. 33 (1967), pp. 589–609.

8. Richard F. Fenno, Jr., *Congressmen in Committees* (Boston: Little, Brown, 1973), p. 64.

9. In late 1969, for example, a federal grand jury indicted Spiegel, Inc. (a major user of third-class mail) and former U.S. Senator Daniel B. Brewster (D., MD, 1963–1968) on charges that Brewster had accepted $24,500 from Spiegel to influence his vote on postal rate legislation. See *Congressional Quarterly Weekly Report*, December 12, 1969, pp. 2548–2549.

10. *Wall Street Journal*, September 20, 1967, p. 3.

11. Richard Fenno, writing in his study of congressional committees about members of the House Post Office and Civil Service Committee, notes: "Neither they nor anyone else in the House perceives these two committees [Post Office and Interior] as providing a source of power and prestige within the House." (Fenno, *Congressmen in Committees*, p. 7).

12. Arthur D. Little, Inc., "Procedural Matters," p. 23.

13. See, for example, U.S., Congress, House, *Postal Revenue Act of 1967, Hearings*, pp. 133, 152, 265, 437, 522, 621, 708.

14. President's Commission on Postal Organization, *Towards Postal Excellence*, Annex, vol. 2, "Rates and Rate-Making," chap. 8, p. 1.

15. *Ibid.*, chap. 1, pp. 2, 3.

16. *United States Code*, Title 39, sec. 3625.

17. Chief Administrative Law Judge Seymour J. Wenner was hearing examiner for the first two rate cases. The rate commission chose not to use a hearing examiner in the third and fourth cases.

18. United States, Postal Rate Commission, "Postal Rate Commission Handbook," mimeographed, December 1976, pp. 10, 13.

19. *United States Code*, Title 39, sec. 3622.

20. Quoted in Bruce E. Thorp, "Postal Report: Mail Users Adjust Lobbying Techniques to Meet New Procedures for Setting Rates," *National Journal*, May 1, 1971, p. 920.

21. U.S. President, Executive Order 11570, "Providing for the Regulation of Conduct for the Postal Rate Commission and Its Employees," *Weekly Compilation of Presidential Documents*, November 30, 1970, pp. 1595–1596.

22. 39 C.F.R. 3000.735

23. 39 C.F.R. 3000.735-501.

24. 39 C.F.R. 3000.735-310.

25. See *Washington Post*, February 21, 1980, p. A10; February 28, 1980, p. B5.

26. Richard Barton, "Postal Rate-Making Explained," *Direct Marketing Journal*, vol. 2, no. 6 (July 1980), p. 7.

27. *Ibid.*
28. John Jay Daly, quoted in Thorp, "Postal Report," p. 928.
29. U.S., Congress, House, Committee on Post Office and Civil Service, *Operation and Organization of the Postal Rate Commission, Hearings before a Subcommittee of the Committee on Post Office and Civil Service,* 93rd Cong., 2d Sess., 1974, p. 31.
30. Thorp, "Postal Report," p. 928.
31. United States Postal Service, *Action of the Governors under 39 U.S.C., Section 3625 and Supporting Record in the Matter of Postal Rate and Fee Increases, 1974: Docket No. R74-1 before the Postal Rate Commission* (Washington: U.S. Government Printing Office, 1975), vol. 1, p. 427.
32. U.S., Congress, House, *Operation and Organization of the Postal Rate Commission, Hearings,* p. 31.
33. Clyde S. DuPont, "The Postal Rate Commission," in Roger Sherman, ed., *Perspectives on Postal Service Issues* (Washington: American Enterprise Institute for Public Policy Research, 1980), p. 115.

Chapter 6

SETTING RATES: COSTING AND PRICING CONTROVERSIES

Although the new institutional and procedural arrangements for setting postal rates are not as highly politicized as rate-setting by Congress, the new process is nevertheless "political." That is, postal rate policy continues to involve matters over which different groups disagree sharply and over which they maneuver for control. This is to be expected whenever decisions about allocating economic resources are at stake. At issue in the continuing controversies are two basic questions: (1) whether the Postal Service has accurately determined the costs it incurs in providing each class of mail service; and (2) whether the rates for the various classes are imposing on them more or less than their legally prescribed share of the system's total costs. There is sharp disagreement on these questions in part because it is difficult to produce the data needed to answer them and those data that exist are by no means incontestable.

The source of the problem here is that the Postal Service is a classic example of an industry that produces more than one output (in this case, different classes or kinds of mail service for letters, parcels, circulars, and so on) through the use of many of the same primary facilities (post offices, delivery vehicles, personnel, and the like). These shared production resources create common costs of production—that is, "institutional costs," which are simply part of making the system itself available and are thus common to all

119

classes of mail. But the presence of these institutional costs greatly complicates determination of the basic cost structure, the correct allocation of costs among the various classes of service, and establishment of an appropriate and generally acceptable set of rates.[1] Hence the continuing controversies.

Background

For much of the postal system's early history, the ingredients for these controversies were missing. Most people used the system for similar purposes and all had roughly the same rate burden.[2] In addition, potential conflicts among mailers over rates were muted because as a general rule in those days, the recipient of a letter paid for it. If he did not want a piece of mail, or could not afford it, he simply did not pay the postmaster for it.[3]

But with the nation's rapid transformation in the nineteenth century from an agrarian economy to an industrial and commercial one, the postal system became more important as a communications and materials-distribution network. Growing mail volume and increasing varieties of mail matter brought heightened demands for different kinds of postal services. This, in turn, created a need for formal rate classifications and rate differentiations. In 1863 Congress finally established three formal classes of mail with different rates. The rate design simplified and reduced postage for printed matter and established a uniform letter rate of three cents a half ounce regardless of distance.[4] From then on, the postal organization was embroiled in continual controversies over the allocation of the postal system's costs among the various classes of mail.

In 1926, in hopes of forestalling further controversies, the Post Office Department established its first formal costing system—the Cost Ascertainment System (CAS)—which fully allocated all costs among the various classes of service.[5] But over the following decades the CAS generated intense disputes, sparking spasmodic efforts both inside and outside the government to find alternative costing systems to replace it.

In 1954 an advisory group for the Senate Post Office and Civil Service Committee severely criticized reliance on the CAS in setting postal rates; the group insisted that the system merely allocated by statistical means the revenues and expenditures to the various classes of mail "on the assumption that each class is as responsible for all of the existing facilities as any other class." The CAS presumed that since many of the facilities must be used jointly, it would be proper to charge each class with its relative share in using the facilities.[6] Fourteen years later, in examining the "irrational postal rate system," the President's Commission on Postal Organization called the CAS "arbitrary" and "uninformative," and complained that the system simply did not generate the functional cost data needed to resolve the historical controversies over whether each class paid its proper rate.[7]

The special mailing industries shared in this desire for a new postal costing system. For years, organized mailers who felt that the CAS imposed unfair rate burdens on them had attacked the system before congressional committees, usually arguing that the CAS allocated to them a disproportionate share of the system's institutional, or common, costs.[8] Some mailers also claimed that the CAS did not take adequate account of the direct costs involved in handling their materials. Third-class mailers, for example, argued that the CAS did not properly credit them for the money they claimed to save the Post Office by presorting their own mail.[9] (The argument on this point was by no means cut and dried. Since cost figures were derived from observations of time spent by clerks handling the various classes of mail, any lower time spent by clerks handling presorted third-class mail presumably showed in the cost figures.) The matter was important to third-class mailers because CAS figures showed their class of service adding to the postal deficit. The situtaion assumed still greater importance for them in 1970, when it became clear that Congress was going to require each class to pay its full costs under a reorganized postal system, thereby causing substantial raises in third-class rates.

Thus, during the early debate on postal reorganization, the third-class mailers pressed not only for a rate-making panel outside the postal corporation, but also for a new costing system. Their objections to the reorganization proposal ceased when it finally became clear that the Post Office was going to adopt a new costing system that would show third-class mail not only to be paying its own way but actually making a profit for the Post Office. Since a general consensus had emerged among cost analysts and postal reformers that the CAS would have to give way to a new system, it would be unfair to suggest that the Post Office adopted new costing methods in

1970 in exchange for third-class mailers' support of the reorganization. Still, the Post Office Department may well have found it difficult to get the reorganization through Congress over the objection of the powerful third-class mail users. Robert M. Huse, executive director of the Mail Advertising Services Association, an organization representing third-class mailers, stated the case moderately: "I think the promise to change the costs system made reform a little more palatable." [10]

Members of Congress also found the new approach satisfying. Although the reorganization would free them from continuing responsibility for setting postal rates, the legislators were still concerned about which costs should be reflected in the rates for each class. When the conference committee in 1970 thrashed out the final version of the reorganization bill, it adopted a Senate provision that contained one of the act's most important standards: "Each class of mail or type of mail service should bear the direct and indirect postal costs attributable to that class plus that portion of other costs of the postal service reasonably assignable to such class or type." [11] In short, the reorganization act directed that each class was thenceforth to pay the costs directly attributable to it plus some share of the system's common, or institutional, costs.

But the act left unspecified (and thus gave the Postal Service discretion in choosing) the methods to be used in calculating the attributable costs and assigning the remaining institutional costs among the various classes of mail. Not surprisingly, there have been continuing conflicts over what costs can actually be identified as having been "caused by" a particular class of mail and thus attributable to it. The Postal Service has chosen costing and pricing methods that have generated much criticism and debate.

Postal Costing and Pricing Methods

In the first three rate cases, the Postal Service used a "short-run" costing method that attributed to mail classes only volume-related costs, leaving out long-run capacity costs. That is, to be attributed to a particular class under this costing method, a cost had to be variable, fluctuating from year to year with changes in the volume of mail in that class. Thus, included in the many costs left unattributed by this short-run costing method were[12]

> . . . all costs for the purchase and lease of buildings, the purchase of
> equipment and vehicles, expenses for vehicle drivers, vehicle mainte-
> nance, building and equipment maintenance and custodial cost, the
> cost of a mailman's driving or walking his route to deliver mail, one-
> third of purchased transportation, most supplies including gasoline
> and oil, and a considerable portion of clerk's time (including window
> service).

Most economists consider expenses such as these to be long-run incremental costs, which under proper costing practices should be assigned to the classes of mail for whose benefit the outlays are
made.[13] But in the first three rate cases, the Postal Service argued
(and the rate commission agreed) that accurate data simply were
not available to permit long-run incremental costing.

It is also true, however, that the Postal Service had no incentive
to move quickly to produce those data. After all, the short-run costing method was attractive because it left between 40 and 51 per
cent of the system's total costs for the Postal Service to "assign"
among the various classes of mail according to its discretion. Since
assigning these unattributed, "institutional" costs allows the Postal
Service room to juggle the total rate burden among the various mail
classes, the methods used in that assignment naturally raise substantial disagreement.

Also controversial is the Postal Service's use of a pricing formula,
developed by two Postal Service economists, that includes three
factors: (1) the estimated elasticity of demand for each class of mail;
(2) the "value" of each class of mail; and (3) the competitive stance
of the Postal Service in those classes in which it lacks a legal monopoly. The first of these factors is purportedly the most important
of the three. That is, postal economists say that they spread the
organization's institutional costs primarily by marking up the marginal cost of each product in inverse proportion to the presumed
elasticity of its demand.[14]

The Postal Service claims that this application of the "inverse
elasticity rule" (IER) is the best available way to find the optimum
rate for each class of mail and service. In theory, the optimum rate
is the rate that maximizes the volume of mail while recovering all
the related attributable costs and making some contribution to the
fixed overhead, so that in the end total costs are recovered. If prices
for each service were set at marginal cost, the Postal Service would
fail to recover its substantial institutional costs. Thus, the Postal
Service uses the IER as a guide in setting prices above marginal

costs to recover the institutional costs, at the same time interfering as little as possible with an economically efficient allocation of resources.[15] Theoretically, that is, in a comparison of two products, if a rate is raised more for the product with a less elastic demand, the change in price will induce proportionately less change in volume than if the rate is raised for a product with a more elastic demand. And the smaller the change from the volumes that would have been in effect if marginal cost prices had prevailed, the smaller the deviation from the economically optimal use that would usually occur at marginal cost prices.[16]

But the application of the IER in postal costing and rate-making has caused controversies because economic theory approves the use of the IER only if two prerequisites are met: (1) the enterprise must be at a stage of productive capacity at which it has decreasing costs with scale; and (2) the correct elasticities of demand must be known and applied.[17]

The Postal Service is not, however, incontestably in accord with either of these criteria. The debate over economies of scale in the postal system is far from being settled one way or another.[18] And as for the second prerequisite, Postal Service economists openly acknowledge that "the techniques for measuring demand elasticity are generally inadequate," holding that "conventional techniques for computing demand elasticity can, at best, provide only approximate indicators of price sensitivity." [19]

Because of this unreliability of the data on the elasticity of demand for various postal services, postal economists have taken what they feel is the "pragmatic course" of ranking the main categories of mail in accordance with *their judgment* of the relative demand elasticity for each class, and then using these rankings as their primary, but not exclusive, basis for assigning unattributed costs among the various classes.

Even if the inverse elasticity rule is appropriate in setting postal rates, its use in conjunction with the short-run costing method has been a recipe for controversy. The net effect of the postal costing and pricing methods has been to permit the Postal Service to place an inappropriate share of the rate burden on first-class mail, which to date has a less elastic demand than other classes largely because the Postal Service has a legal monopoly over it. The short-run incremental costing method leaves an extraordinary share of the postal system's total costs in the "fixed" cost category, thus providing the

Postal Service with more discretion in assigning all those costs (from one half to one third the entire postal budget) however it likes. For example, by defining long-run costs as fixed or institutional costs, and then distributing them among the various classes by reference to the inverse elasticity rule, the Postal Service allows itself to charge the cost of, say, a new facility to classes of mail that may not even be processed by that facility. This is what happened in the case of the new billion-dollar National Bulk Mail System, built by the Postal Service between 1971 and 1976 to handle bulk third- and fourth-class mail and some second-class mail. Because the Postal Service's short-run costing method classifies buildings and equipment as "fixed" costs, the Postal Service is able to charge 58 per cent of the costs of this bulk-mail system to first-class mail, even though none of these facilities is used to handle first-class mail.[20]

Challenges to the Methods

Naturally, these costing and pricing methods adopted by the Postal Service and sanctioned by the Postal Rate Commission have not gone unchallenged. Indeed, they have been a principal source of controversy in the postal policy arena throughout the 1970s, as the chief administrative law judge of the PRC and federal appeals courts have successively ruled that the methods fail to comply with the provisions of the Postal Reorganization Act.

Postal reformers in 1970 had anticipated that a more independent postal organization might be inclined to push an unfair portion of the cost burden onto first-class mailers. The Senate Post Office and Civil Service Committee, for example, explicitly acknowledged that "the temptation to resolve the financial problems of the Post Office by charging the lion's share of all operating costs to first-class mail is strong; that's where the big money is." [21] And it was with an eye toward preventing that imposition on first-class mailers that the Postal Reorganization Act contained a requirement that the Postal Rate Commission should appoint an Officer of the Commission (OOC) "to represent the interests of the general public" in proceedings before the commission.[22]

The OOC, assisted by attorneys and rate analysts, has found in the rate proceedings that the Postal Service is relying too much on judgmental factors in setting rates. Use of the inverse elasticity rule as a guide in assigning institutional costs is, in the OOC's view, "not supported by law, nor by economics, nor by basic factual data."[23]

But even stronger (and more important) criticisms of the Postal Service's cost-accounting and assignment has come from Seymour J. Wenner, the rate commission's chief administrative law judge, who acted as hearing examiner in the first two rate cases following the reorganization. Wenner had been a hearing examiner for the Federal Power Commission for the ten years before he was hired by the PRC; he had also for several years been hearing examiner for the Interstate Commerce Commission and chief counsel to the Civil Aeronautics Board. In the initial decision he rendered in the first rate case, Wenner criticized the Postal Service's loose approach to cost attribution and its judgmental cost assignments. "Distributing billions of dollars on the basis of thinly supported judgments is not an acceptable method," he wrote. "And it is an invitation to pressures which Congress sought to avoid."[24] Citing specific cases in which theory failed to appear in practice, Wenner examined the Postal Service's efforts to include in the cost assignment formula some assessment of the *value* of different classes of mail to the recipients, and he concluded:[25]

> *Here, Postal Service becomes involved in social considerations and subjective evaluations which are difficult to apply. For example, Postal Service finds that the contents of second-class mail have a high value because of their "cultural, educational, and informational values," which justify a* low *price. . . . But as has been noted, Postal Service deems the contents of first-class to have a high value which warrants a* high *price.*

Moreover, Wenner criticized the Postal Service's cost attribution and cost assignment methods on several predictable grounds. He held that they inadequately reflected the costs each class of mail imposed on the system; they increased future cost and rate instability by not taking present account of predictable long-run cost variability; and they enlarged the amount of institutional costs distributed to the classes of mail on the basis of the Postal Service's judgmental evaluation of pricing factors instead of on a cost basis.[26]

But Wenner acknowledged the difficulties the Postal Service faced in developing all new costing data and rate-design techniques for the first case, and he contented himself for the time with recommending that the assignment of costs on a judgmental basis be reduced in future rate proposals by a more diligent effort to link long-term and indirect costs to the classes of service that give rise to them.[27]

When the Postal Rate Commission formally issued its recommended decision in this first rate case to the Postal Board of Governors, the commissioners tried to soften Wenner's criticisms by acknowledging the difficulties the Postal Service faced because of the novelty of the proceedings, the dearth of reliable data, and the limited amount of time available for preparation. But the rate commissioners also admitted there was much truth to Wenner's complaints and promised that the commission itself would prepare rules to deal with the Postal Service's deficient accounting and cost-assignment techniques.[28]

The rate schedule produced in the first rate case brought the Postal Service another challenge (this time in federal court) by the Association of American Publishers and other organizations that felt that the rates had been unfairly increased for special fourth-class mail (books, films, sound recordings, and the like), while parcel post rates were left untouched. The court denied and dismissed the petitioners' request that the rates be set aside but used the opportunity to comment on the Potal Service's cost-accounting and assignment practices. Chief Judge David Bazelon, joined by Circuit Judge Edward A. Tamm and Senior District Judge Charles E. Wyzanski, Jr., wrote that the Postal Service had "some distance to go" to reach the objectives of postal reform. The court characterized the Postal Service's response to the rate guidelines established by the reorganization act as "questionable at best." And the judges also criticized the Service's pricing formula on the grounds that it vested "an unstructured and well-nigh unreviewable discretion in two individuals [the postal economists who originated the formula] to propose allocation of over half the Service's budget." The court also held that discretionary or "reasonable" assignment of costs should apply only when the Postal Service absolutely could not attribute costs. For the Postal Service to correct its errors, the court said, it would have to "itemize its costs in more detail, determine which classes of service caused them, and attribute those costs solely on that basis. Only very long-term costs and overhead could be 'reasonably assigned.'" [29]

In spite of Wenner's earlier warnings and those of the court, the Postal Service appeared for the second rate case in 1973 with the same low level of attributable costs and the same discretionary pricing formula. The hearing examiner was upset. In advising the Postal Rate Commission why he thought it should reject the Postal Service's new rate request, Wenner wrote:[30]

The Postal Service has become a tax-collecting agency, collecting money from first-class mailers to distribute to other favored classes. Every time a person pays 10 cents to mail a first-class letter he is paying his appropriate attributable share of residual costs, and in addition, he is contributing almost 2 cents to pay the costs of other services.

The hearing examiner argued that if the Postal Service would not remedy its own deficient cost determinations and attributions, then the commission should do it: "The task is no longer to criticize and exhort; it is to do the job—now." [31]

With that introduction, Wenner rendered an initial decision on May 28, 1975, that set off shock waves throughout the nation's mailing community. In a detailed decision, Wenner proposed a drastic redistribution of the cost burden among the various classes of mail, lowering the cost for a first-class stamp (from the 10-cent rate the Postal Service had temporarily established, to 8.5 cents), and increasing substantially the rates for the other classes.[32] The greatest fear Wenner's decision touched off was inside the Postal Service itself and in the hearts (and expressed on the editorial pages) of magazine publishers reliant on second-class mail.

The Postal Service viewed the Wenner proposal as a threat to its own survival and urged the Postal Rate Commission to reject the judge's rate proposals, claiming that Wenner's recommended rates would force second-, third-, and fourth-class mail users to find alternatives to the postal system, and would therefore eventually lead to much higher costs to the remaining users of the system, especially first-class mailers.[33]

The second-class mailers let out an even more emotional howl. For example, the *New York Times*, far more sedate in its response than most publications, scored the Wenner proposal, holding that an increase in second-class rates would eventually deprive the public of the information disseminated through magazines, newspapers, and other publications.[34] Most other publications pounded on the same theme, although framing the case much more vividly. *Time*, one of the postal system's largest mail users, predicted that to meet increased postage costs, most publications would have to increase dramatically their subscription rates, raising magazine prices beyond the reach of many: "To survive, publications would need not simply loyal but also rich readers." [35] The second-class mailers held up the specter of thousands of magazines and newspapers folding under the burden of increased postage rates. While executives of the Magazine Publishers Association acknowledged that the larger, richer publications would survive under the Wenner plan, they claimed that the real threat was to smaller magazines, mail-delivered newspapers, and intellectual journals of opinion.[36] These arguments echoed Arthur Schlesinger, Jr.'s earlier warning that increasing second-class rates were making the Postal Service "the judge, jury, and executioner of the nation's intellectual life." [37]

For weeks following Judge Wenner's proposal, the Postal Rate Commission worked through the briefs submitted by the Postal Service and by the intervenors in exception to the examiner's initial decision. Following three months of sustained appeals from mailers, the commission issued its recommended decision, rejecting the Wenner proposal. Though the rate commission produced cost attributions 16 per cent higher than those produced by the Postal Service, the PRC failed to go beyond that, claiming that the record provided inadequate basis for doing more. And although the PRC admonished the Postal Service to present better data in the future or face the possibility of having its rate requests rejected, the commission accepted the Postal Service's costing methods once again.[38]

Less than three weeks later, on September 18, 1975, the Postal Service initiated the third postal rate case, submitting a request to the rate commission with cost data attributing only slightly greater cost attributions than in previous cases. Though the rate request called for higher rates in each class, it proposed an extraordinary hike for first-class rates from 10 cents to 13 cents an ounce. Moreover, the rate commissioners announced that they would hear this rate case themselves, thereby removing from the scene the first-class mail users' chief defender, Judge Wenner.

By this time, the handwriting was on the wall for all parties to see; the rate commission apparently had no intention of rejecting or seriously modifying postal rate requests, thus leaving the Postal Service effectively in control over its own rate structure. Rates were sure to continue to climb, moreover, since the Postal Service was demonstrably failing to control costs. The National Association of Greeting Card Publishers—an organization with obvious concerns over soaring first-class rates—was alarmed by these trends and stung by the decision in the second rate case. It turned to the U.S. Court of Appeals for review of the Postal Service's rate decisions. The court's opinion, finally issued on December 28, 1976, sent another shock wave through the postal community. The court held that the Postal Service's methods of costing and setting rates "fail to comply with the act," and the judges rendered invalid and illegal the methodologies used by the Postal Service and endorsed by the rate commission. The court, praising the cost-attribution methods used by Seymour Wenner in his controversial proposal, said that the costing methods of the Postal Service had failed to attribute enough costs directly to the classes of mail.[39] The decision in the *Greeting Cards* case turned out to be an important catalyst, forcing the Postal Service and the PRC to find ways of increasing cost attributions.

Because of a continuing rise in total operating costs, the Postal Service needed a new rate increase and began preparing a rate request in early 1977. Though the Service had little choice but to increase its cost attributions, it took this step with understandable reluctance. The users of second-, third-, and fourth-class mail could be expected to look more earnestly for alternative delivery methods. But knowing that a continuation of its former cost-accounting practices would be rejected in the courts, the Postal Service and the rate commission applied a new "service-related cost" concept, enabling them to identify certain fixed mail delivery costs that are caused by the need to maintain a delivery system six days a week rather than three days a week.[40] The effect of the modified costing methods was apparent in the PRC's recommended decision; attributable and assignable cost together accounted for 74.5 per cent of the total revenue requirement.[41]

Yet it appears that the Postal Service and the rate commission so far have done little to end the placing of an inappropriate share of the rate burden on first-class mail to cross-subsidize other classes. Although the appeals court disapproved of further use of the inverse elasticity rule, the Postal Service and the rate commission continue to apply it implicitly. At the start of the fourth rate case, for example, Edward J. McCaffrey, the general manager of the Postal Service's rate design division, explained the Postal Service's assignment of a minimal amount of institutional costs to second-class mail by pointing to the threatened diversions of mail from that class to private delivery systems.[42] In short, the method for setting rates above attributable costs continues in the same way as in the past—by ranking the categories of mail in accordance with judgments about the relative demand elasticity for each class and then using these rankings as the primary basis for assigning unattributed costs. Thus, first-class mail continues to bear the great percentage of the system's institutional costs.

The rate-makers' stubborn persistence in this practice is easy to understand by immediate considerations. They fear that if rates for second-, third-, and fourth-class mail increase sharply, the users of these classes will look more earnestly for alternative delivery methods and also beseech Congress to increase federal subsidies to the Postal Service to slow the rate of increase in postage prices; these prospects are clearly anathema to postal executives.

Yet the chosen pricing policies of the Postal Service and the PRC are less understandable in view of long-term considerations. Over time, placing the extra burden on first-class mailers will surely be self-defeating because very high rates will encourage these mailers (mostly businesses) to find alternative means of message transmission—a move facilitated (as the next chapter shows) by revolutionary developments in electronic communications.

Endnotes

1. Melvyn A. Fuss, "Cost Allocation: How Can the Costs of Postal Services Be Determined?" in Roger Sherman, ed., *Perspectives on Postal Service Issues* (Washington: American Enterprise Institute for Public Policy Research, 1980), p. 30.
2. Newspapers did enjoy a slightly preferential rate. U.S., Post Office Department, *United States Domestic Postage Rates, 1789–1956* (Washington: U.S. Government Printing Office, 1956), p. 21.
3. Gerald Cullinan, *The Post Office Department* (New York: Frederick A. Praeger, Publishers, 1968), p. 28. As Cullinan notes, at the high rates prevailing in the early years of the postal system, the recipient of a letter "could but hope that his expensive correspondents had something to say" (p. 28).
4. U.S., Post Office Department, *Domestic Postage Rates, 1789–1956*, pp. 8, 21.
5. For a full explanation of the cost ascertainment system, see U.S., President's Commission on Postal Organization, Report of the Commission, *Towards Postal Excellence* (Washington: U.S. Government Printing Office, 1968), Annex, vol. 2, "Rates and Rate-Making," chap. 4, pp. 4-8 to 4-24; see also vol. 2, "Cost Accounting for Classes of Postal Service."
6. U.S., Congress, Senate, Committee on Post Office and Civil Service, *Postal Rates and Postal Policy of the Post Office Department*, S. Rept. 1086, 83rd Cong., 2d Sess., 1954, p. 21.

7. President's Commission on Postal Organization, *Towards Postal Excellence*, p. 30.
8. See U.S., Congress, House, Committee on Post Office and Civil Service, *Post Office Cost Ascertainment System, Hearings before a Subcommittee of the Committee on Post Office and Civil Service*, 91st Cong., 1st Sess., 1969, p. 92.
9. *Washington Post*, June 11, 1974, p. A1.
10. *Ibid.*, p. A6.
11. *United States Code*, Title 39, sec. 3622(b)(3). See U.S. Congress, House, Committee on Conference, *Postal Reorganization*, Conference Report No. 91-1363, 91st Cong., 2d Sess., 1970, p. 87.
12. "Chief Administrative Law Judge's Initial Decision," in United States Postal Service, *Action of the Governors under 39 U.S.C., Section 3625, and Supporting Record in the Matter of Postal Rate and Fee Increases, 1974: Docket No. R74-1 before the Postal Rate Commission* (Washington: U.S. Government Printing Office, 1975), vol. 1, p. 1-3.
13. See Alfred E. Kahn, *The Economics of Regulation*, 2 vols. (New York: John Wiley and Sons, 1970), vol. 1, chap. 4.
14. For postal economists' explanation of their use of the inverse elasticity rule, see Postal Rate Commission, *Postal Rate and Fee Increases*, Docket R76-1, vol. 1, *Opinion and Recommended Decision* (Washington: Postal Rate Commission, 1977), pp. 123–125, 138.
15. *Ibid.*
16. Kahn, *Economics of Regulation*, vol. 1, p. 144.
17. *Ibid.*, pp. 142–150.
18. For example, a 1961 study by Morton Baratz concluded that long-run postal costs for all classes of mail were probably still in the decreasing range and that if some functions could be mechanized (this *has* happened), the costs would remain in the decreasing range for some time to come. Baratz, *Economics of the Postal Service* (Washington: Public Affairs Press, 1962), pp. 30–33.

   On the other side of the argument, Rodney E. Stevenson's time-series analysis, using data covering the years 1961–1971, produced results indicating that the postal system does not operate under decreasing costs; some of Stevenson's equations even suggest that the postal system realizes *increasing* costs with scale. Rodney E. Stevenson, "Postal Pricing Problems and Production Functions" (Ph.D. dissertation, Michigan State University, 1973). See also Stevenson's testimony before the Postal Rate Commission in *Postal Rate and Fee Increases, Docket R74-1*, vol. 4, pp. 1332–1425.

   A 1968 study by Foster Associates and Ernst & Ernst for the President's Commission on Postal Organization concluded that the data on this subject remain "limited and inconclusive." On the basis of the existing data, they believed, however, that "the postal service is subjected to decreasing unit costs with increasing scale." President's Commission on Postal Organization, *Towards Postal Excellence* (Washington: U.S. Government Printing Office, 1968), vol. 2, "Rates and Rate-Making," chap. 1, p. 1-3.
19. Arthur Eden, in direct testimony before the Postal Rate Commission, in *Postal Rate and Fee Increases, Docket R74-1*, vol. 3, part 1, p. 3-37, col. 1; p. 3-32, col. 3.

20. "Chief Administrative Law Judge's Initial Decision," in *Postal Rate and Fee Increases, Docket R74-1*, vol. 1, p. 1-3. The Postal Service apparently alters its costing methods depending on the purpose to which the data are being put. For example, the Postal Service's feasibility studies, on the basis of which the decision was made to invest in the expensive bulk-mail system, treated its cost as a *long-term* incremental cost. (See CALJ's initial decision in *Postal Rate and Fee Increases, Docket R74-1*, vol. 1, p. 1-3, col. 3, note 1.)

21. U.S., Congress, Senate, Committee on Post Office and Civil Service, *Postal Reorganization*, S. Rept. No. 91-912, 91st Cong., 2d Sess., 1970, p. 13.

22. *United States Code*, Title 39, sec. 3624(a).

23. Brief of Assistant General Counsel, Litigation Division, Postal Rate Commission, to Presiding Examiner, in United States Postal Service, *Action of the Governors under 39 U.S.C., Section 3625, and Supporting Record in the Matter of Postal Rate and Fee Increases, 1971: Docket No. R71-1 before the Postal Rate Commission* (Washington: U.S. Government Printing Office, 1972), vol. 2, part 2, p. 717. The Officer of the Commission wrote: "If there is any pricing basis that a public service organization such as the U.S. Postal Service should *not* adopt, it is the inverse elasticity theory" (p. 718).

24. "Chief Administrative Law Judge's Initial Decision," in *Postal Rate and Fee Increases, Docket R71-1*, vol. 1, p. 1-17.

25. *Ibid.*, p. 1–14.

26. *Ibid.*, p. 1–7.

27. *Ibid.*, p. 1–17.

28. "Opinion and Recommended Decision of the Postal Rate Commission," in *Postal Rate and Fee Increases, Docket R71-1*, vol. 1, p. 268.

29. *Association of American Publishers, Inc., et. al. v. The Governors of the United States Postal Service.* 485 F. 2d 768 (1973), pp. 777–779.

30. "Chief Administrative Law Judge's Initial Decision," in *Postal Rate and Fee Increases, Docket R74-1*, vol. 1, p. 1-4

31. *Ibid.*

32. *Ibid.*, pp. 1-3 to 1-32.

33. U.S., Postal Service, General Release No. 53, June 17, 1975.

34. *New York Times*, June 7, 1975, p. 26.

35. *Time*, June 16, 1975, p. 45.

36. *New York Times*, June 16, 1975, p. 45.

37. *Wall Street Journal*, January 31, 1974, p. 12.

38. "Opinion and Recommended Decision of the Postal Rate Commission," in *Postal Rate and Fee Increases, Docket R74-1*, vol. 1, pp. 1-612 to 1-614.

39. *National Association of Greeting Card Publishers v. United States Postal Service*, 569 F. 2d 570 (D.C. Cir., December 28, 1976).

40. U.S., Postal Rate Commission, *Postal Rate and Fee Increases: Opinion and Recommended Decision*, Docket R77-1 (Washington: Postal Rate Commission, May 12, 1978), pp. 94–101.

41. *Ibid.*, p. 93.

42. U.S., Postal Service, Request of the United States Postal Service for a Recommended Decision on Changes in Rates and Fees for Postal Services, July 1977; testimony of Edward J. McCaffrey, Exhibit USPS-T-76, p. 13.

Chapter 7

THE POSTAL SERVICE FACES COMPETITION

In the decade since 1970, the reconstituted Postal Service has faced profound changes in its environment. Most of the changes are the consequence of provisions in the Postal Reorganization Act that led to significant alterations in the relationship of the Postal Service to Congress, the White House, the postal unions, and the principal mailing industries. But one of the most important changes in the Postal Service's managerial environment was not a direct effect of the reorganization—the rapid stiffening of competition in many of its service classes, and the particularly threatening development of new electronic communications systems.

Competition itself is nothing new to the postal system. For years, the mail agency has faced competition from private firms in the conveyance of small parcels and from newspapers and the broadcast media for advertisers' business. Moreover, ever since the telephone came into widespread use, serving as a readily available substitute for many kinds of mail communication, the postal system has found its share of the total message-communications market sharply diminishing.

But the fast-growing competition in the years since the reorganization is especially important because it threatens to divert billions of pieces of mail each year from the postal system, with serious consequences for the future operation and financing of the mail system. We now examine what these new competitive pressures are and why concern over the competition posed by the electronic communications revolution is overshadowing the age-old debate about repealing the postal system's monopoly on letter mail.

Alternative Systems for Delivering Material

Although the postal system has had a legal monopoly on the delivery of first-class letters ever since 1845, the government's mail agency has long faced competitive pressures in its other services. In recent decades, the postal system has faced substantial competition from (1) firms that specialize in delivering small parcels; (2) firms that deliver advertising material and magazines; and (3) companies (especially utilities) that use their own employees to deliver bills.

Small Parcels

To date, the stiffest competition the Postal Service faces in any of its service classes has come in the small-parcel market, which includes all parcels or packages weighing up to 50 pounds. Many private firms in the United States now compete in the surface parcel and air parcel markets. In addition to the package services of the two main bus lines—Greyhound and Continental Trailways—and the thousands of local and regional private package-delivery services, the ranks of competitors in the small-parcel market include fast-growing firms specializing in the high-priority air parcel market. An example of a company that is doing well in this air parcel market is the Federal Express Corporation, based in Memphis, which started operating in 1972. Federal Express has built a formidable corporate empire around an overnight package-delivery service. As of May 1979, Federal Express's "integrated air-ground transportation system" included 80 to 90 planes, roughly 1,500 delivery vans, and full-service offices in 114 cities. For its fiscal year ending May 31, 1979, Federal Express reported operating revenues of $235.5 million and a net income of $21.4 million.[1] Also competing in the transportation of high-priority, time-sensitive materials are various air freight forwarders such as Emery, Airborne, and Purolator Courier.

By far the most important of the Postal Service's competitors in the small-parcel market is the United Parcel Service (UPS). Founded in 1907, UPS has gradually developed its role as a seriously competitive common carrier. From its inception as a messenger service in Seattle, the company moved into retail delivery of small parcels for department stores. It then began its common-carrier service in earnest for industrial and commercial shippers following World War II, as retailing patterns shifted with the proliferation of the suburbs and the declining importance of downtown department stores.[2]

In recent years, UPS has captured the most attractive segment of the small-parcel shipment market once dominated by the Postal Service. In fact, parcel shippers have deserted the Postal Service for UPS in droves. The Postal Service's annual parcel volume fell dramatically from 725 million parcels in 1968 to 447 million in 1978. Its parcel revenues in the same period fell from $649 million to $417 million. The United Parcel Service, on the other hand, increased dramatically its volume in the same period, from 404 million to 1.3 billion packages. Its revenues soared from $355 million to $2.7 billion.[3]

The Postal Service has lost this parcel business in spite of its expenditure of $1 billion for the development of the national network of bulk-mail processing centers (described in Chapter 3). Two immediate factors help account for the diversion of parcel business to UPS. First, market research conducted by the Postal Service reveals that parcel shippers care more about predictability and consistency of delivery than about speed. And as the evidence indicates (Chapter 3), parcel delivery by the Postal Service is neither speedy nor predictable and consistent. Business firms contacted by General Accounting Office investigators reported that UPS provides faster, more consistent, and more highly predictable parcel delivery than the Postal Service does.[4]

An even more important reason for the parcel volume diversion to UPS is the lower rates charged by the private firm. The same GAO study found that for most businesses that send large volumes of parcels, cost is the primary factor in determining how to ship them. Current parcel post rates simply are not competitive with the rates UPS charges, so most firms that produce large volumes of parcels use UPS, especially since it is also superior in speed and predictability of delivery.[5]

These problems facing the Postal Service's parcel operation are interrelated and constitute a cycle of cumulative deterioration for its parcel business. Declining parcel post volumes result in higher processing costs for each parcel. These higher unit costs in turn lead to higher parcel post rates. But as the rates increase, and become even less competitive with UPS, still more parcel business is driven away from the Postal Service, leading to the cumulative deterioration of that service line.

There are still other reasons why the Postal Service has been consistently losing the parcel business to UPS. To be sure, UPS is an aggressive, well-managed, efficient firm. But perhaps more important, the political demands on the government's parcel post service prevent it from being an effective competitor. For example, unlike UPS, which is free to accept only what it wants (and it wants only what it can handle efficiently), the Postal Service must handle a wide variety of shipments from occasional customers as well as from regular shippers. Whereas the Postal Service, in one official's words, has to "ship Aunt Minnie's cookies to her grandchildren even if she doesn't wrap them very well and if the kids live on top of a mountain," UPS deals largely with business firms.[6] Since UPS is often on a contract basis as well, it thus has several clear advantages over the Postal Service; the parcels it handles usually come well packaged, a substantial amount of its volume involves highly concentrated business-to-business and city-to-city traffic, and the company can devise the most efficient pickup routes for its drivers well in advance. Unlike the Postal Service, which is required by political demands to maintain 40,000 facilities for accepting parcels and other mail, UPS maintains a lean network of approximately 1,000 facilities. In the Postal Service, the sites of most of its facilities are chosen for the convenience of patrons. United Parcel, on the other hand, is under no compulsion to choose its sites for the convenience of the shipper. Although UPS will accept packages over the counter, its facilities consist largely of distribution points and truck terminals for its own fleet, so convenience to business and residential areas is not a key factor in choosing facility locations.[7]

The two parcel-delivery operations also face dramatically different operating environments in several other respects. United Parcel Service has sustained some prolonged strikes in order to get acceptable labor contracts. The Postal Service, on the other hand, is highly vulnerable to the wage demands of its employees and (although this may be changing as the public tires of public-employee militancy) would likely find it impossible to outlast its employees in a strike. Moreover, members of Congress do not stop UPS from closing facilities, nor do congressmen and citizens get upset when UPS chooses to deliver to certain neighborhoods on alternate days.[8]

In short, the government's parcel-delivery operation must bear the burden of assorted uneconomical, deficit-creating social obligations, while UPS is free to skim the cream of the parcel market by tailoring its operations to the profitable, large-volume, business-related parcel market in and between urban areas.

Magazine Delivery

With much the same business strategy, other, newer firms have recently begun to compete with the Postal Service in delivering other kinds of material, such as national newspapers, magazines, advertising circulars, and product samples. As postage prices have soared (especially in second class, in which rates have increased by roughly 500 percent between 1970 and 1978), large mail users have increasingly turned to less expensive, private delivery firms. For example, the *Wall Street Journal* for years relied primarily on the postal system for same-day delivery of that paper, but the *Journal* now reportedly has over 240,000 copies a day delivered by private carriers in 82 locations. Other big publications turning to private delivery firms include *Good Housekeeping, Better Homes & Gardens, Ladies' Home Journal, McCall's, Newsweek, Sports Illustrated, Time,* and *U.S. News and World Report.* Large book and record firms such as Book-of-the-Month, Reader's Digest Books, Time-Life Books, Columbia House, and RCA Record Clubs are also using private delivery systems where possible.[9]

Although reliable data are not available, the amount of mail volume diverted by these private delivery systems still is fairly small—probably less than 1 per cent of the total Postal Service volume. But the Service stands to lose more publishers to the competing services as postal subsidies for magazines are completely phased out and as rates continue to increase.

The private delivery firms are winning business away from the Postal Service largely by offering services at a lower price. One reason private carrier firms are able to do this is that they typically focus their attention exclusively on high-density metropolitan areas. This is a particular advantage to carriers of unaddressed advertising circulars that are going to every residence in an area (the equivalent of the Postal Service's third-class "junk mail"). The president of one such concern, the American Postal Service of Opa-Locka, Florida, explains: "We go into a populated area with twelve men on a van and go through it like locusts covering everything there. If we had to stop and look at addresses, it would slow us down quite a bit." [10] It would also increase their costs.

A second characteristic of many of these new private delivery firms is that their carrier forces usually consist of part-time employees—people who want supplementary income, especially students, housewives, retirees, and moonlighters. Thus, although these firms tend to be highly labor-intensive, compensation costs for persons in this so-called "secondary labor force" are much lower than those shouldered by the Postal Service for its full-time, unionized employees. [11]

Utilities' Hand-Delivery Forces

In addition to the competitive pressures on its second-class (newspapers and magazines) and third-class (largely advertising) delivery services, the Postal Service recently has faced increasing competition from large companies, especially public utilities, that hand-deliver their own bills. To many companies with large monthly billings, the increase in first-class postage rates from 6 cents in 1971 to 15 cents in 1978 meant substantial increases in mailing expenses. To minimize this cost, some companies (again, especially utilities) started using their own employees to deliver bills by hand in concentrated areas of the larger cities they serve. In 1979, for example, among the large utilities using their own employees to deliver monthly bills were Peoples Gas (Chicago), the Massachusetts Electric Company, Kansas Gas and Electric Company, Florida Power and Light Company, and the Public Service Electric and Gas Company of New Jersey. [12]

All the competitive delivery schemes described so far are legally permitted under the private express statutes, the body of laws that prohibit private carriage of letters. But some firms have tried to offer services reserved by law to the Postal Service, thus leading to several widely publicized court cases. In one instance, the Independent Postal Service of America (a firm describing itself as "the Avis of the Post Office") sought to deliver addressed Christmas cards within certain cities and to sell private postage stamps to its customers. A district court enjoined the IPSA from continuing the operation. [13] In another, more celebrated case, the Postal Service won a federal court injunction against the P. H. Brennan Hand Delivery Service, run by a Rochester, New York, couple who offered same-day or overnight delivery services to local businesses, charging five cents less per letter than the Postal Service.[14] News accounts of these and similar cases typically cast the Postal Service as a governmental leviathan, stifler of private initiative, and protector not of the public interest but of its own bureaucratic domain.

Repealing the Private Express Statutes

The apparent ability and willingness of some private firms to compete with the Postal Service in some kinds of delivery has cast attention anew on one of the more fervently proposed panaceas for the operating and financial difficulties of the postal system—repeal of the private express statutes. Free-market economists long have called for such a move and recently have advanced this nostrum with increased assuredness.[15] On the surface their arguments seem appealing.

The primary contention of free-market economists is that repealing the Postal Service's monopoly on letter mail delivery would allow a more efficient allocation of economic resources. A monopolized service, so this argument goes, is harmful to the public interest because it leads to unnecessarily high prices for the consumer. In the most thorough recent argument for the monopoly's repeal, economist John Haldi has asserted that competition would have salutary effects since it would lead to cost reductions, would "force rates to levels somewhat more consistent with costs," and would reduce the overcharging of some users of first-class mail. Haldi also argues that if the monopoly were eliminated, any potential competitor, to attract business, would have to beat the Postal Service's rates or provide better letter delivery service at the same rates. But in either case, this competitor would have to "keep his operating costs (including taxes) below those of the Postal Service (which does not pay taxes) in order to earn the necessary profit." [16]

But if the monopoly should be repealed, the most likely event is (as even Haldi admits) that the profit motive would lead private entrepreneurs to serve only the most lucrative portions of the market for letter-mail delivery. This process of identifying and then serving only the more profitable (lower-cost) markets is known as "cream skimming." The most lucrative of all the "cream" in today's postal system is the first-class mail that is mass-produced by computer; this category includes bank statements, bills for bank charge cards, bills from utility companies and department stores, and the like. The sender's computer may even be programmed to produce the mailable items by order of Zip Code or by individual carrier route.[17]

This mail is therefore relatively inexpensive to handle. This is why some utilities have taken to using their regular, full-time employees for delivering bills by hand in concentrated areas of the larger cities they serve. The law permits this particular practice, but removing the broader private express restrictions would compound the Postal Service losses of this desirable local mail volume. Entrepreneurs in every large metropolitan area would cash in on the profit opportunity inherent in relatively easy and inexpensive local delivery of monthly bills and financial statements for local companies.

As cream skimmers expanded their operations to handle, say, billings from large oil companies, and as large-volume mailers sought out these cheaper, more specialized services, the resulting diversion of volume and revenues away from the Postal Service would be substantial. A conservative estimate by McKinsey & Co. in 1973 suggested that the Postal Service could lose about 4.7 billion pieces and $420 million in revenues annually on a nationwide basis to cream skimmers of this type.[18] The likely losses, especially in light of continually rising postal rates, would be much greater. Just as the cream-skimming by UPS has left the government's duty-bound parcel post operation in a shambles, so too the inevitable cream-skimming of first-class letter mail would leave the Postal Service with only the most expensive, least productive segment of the letter-delivery market—such as Aunt Minnie's occasional birthday cards to her nephews in Dinosaur, Colorado. The increasing unit costs of handling this remaining mail would force postal rates up very rapidly unless Congress chose to step in with massive subsidies to the Postal Service.

Just as in the case of its parcel post operation, the Postal Service could not compete effectively after repeal of the monopoly unless it were free to adjust services and rates to reflect market conditions, not political and social demands. For instance, Congress would have to drop its requirement that the Postal Service charge uniform postage on first-class letters regardless of the distance sent or the circumstances of their origin or destination. That is, the Service would have to be free to set its rates to reflect the difference in unit costs occasioned by delivery to and from remote rural areas and maybe even the cost differences between delivery to single-family houses in the suburbs and large apartment buildings in the city. (One need only reflect on the inevitable administrative complexity of such a rate structure to understand why such a move is unlikely.)

Moreover, the Postal Service would have to be free to alter its service structure by, for example, pruning its network of uneconomical rural post offices or reducing deliveries to three days a week. If the Postal Service were not freed from the political demands and statutory constraints that prohibit it from taking these and similar steps, free-market competition in letter-mail delivery would, in one observer's words, be "less competition than cannibalism." [19] The only alternative, after all, would offer only very short-term survival; the Postal Service could continue to increase postage rates for its remaining customers, but these price hikes would quickly induce the same cycle of cumulative deterioration in mail volume that the Postal Service has witnessed in its parcel business.

Either way, the central policy question (though inadequately considered by the advocates of the monopoly's repeal) seems to be who should pay the increased costs on low-volume letter mail, and through what method. The economists have produced one answer; to be fair, the costs should be borne by the users, and rates should be based on costs. Simply identify the marginal costs of the services and increase the rates accordingly.

But this answer fails to indicate a clear financing solution for two reasons. First, setting costs at marginal prices does not recover all the system's costs; it leaves a substantial, unrecovered "fixed," or institutional, cost. (As the previous chapter showed, the Postal Service has been recovering these institutional costs by a second-best solution, adopting a variation of the inverse elasticity rule. This method recovers the institutional costs of the postal system by setting prices above marginal cost in inverse relation to the presumed elasticity of demand for the various services.) Second, economists are concerned not only with basing rates on costs, but also with eliminating cross-subsidization between or within services. But the current method of postal financing, namely charging mailers, contains a strong though generally overlooked element of cross-subsidization; it assumes that the *users* of the system are the *senders* of mail and that the method of paying for the system's fixed costs should be through charges exacted from them. Yet it is clear that a significant portion of the fixed costs of the Postal Service involves maintaining a delivery network to all households and businesses. Most of these costs are incurred regardless of the volume of mail handled. Thus, if the free-market economists' call for cost-based charges is to be met, these customer network charges should be borne, at least partly, by *recipients* of the mail and not just the senders.[20]

By these considerations, there appear to be several alternative methods of financing high-cost, low-volume services besides simply raising rates so high that Aunt Minnie pays more for the stamp than for the birthday card.

First, the delivery network costs could be charged directly to mail recipients through a fixed annual delivery charge to all addresses. This approach would entail several conspicuous problems of equity and efficiency. Devising a fair charge would not be easy. The fee could be based, for example, on the statistical relation between the total number of addresses and total delivery network costs. But this approach would be unfair since it would charge all addresses a uniform fee even though a uniform fee would not reflect variations either in cost per address or in the value received by different recipients. There are, after all, significant cost differences among delivery to a post office box, an apartment house mailbox, a suburban residence, and a mountain cabin. Apart from these "topographical" inequities inherent in a uniform fee, it is also clear that not all residents have the same ability to pay a uniform fee for mail delivery.[21]

There are also efficiency considerations related to the cost of collecting the fee. If the Postal Service tried to collect $2.3 billion in delivery network costs (the estimate for 1977) from its 80 million or so addresses, this would mean about $30 a year from each. The cost of record-keeping, billing, and collecting could amount to so much that any gain from the fee would be obviated, particularly since about 17 per cent of all household addresses change each year.[22]

An alternative financing method would be to help defray the higher cost of providing low-volume delivery (especially the rural delivery) through general tax support. That is, Congress could simply appropriate to the Postal Service the total amount of network delivery costs, in effect providing an open, direct subsidy for the Postal Service to maintain a universal delivery capacity and to provide high-cost services in rural areas. Though this tax-financed method would entail none of the high administrative costs of a direct fee, the substantial economic and redistributive effect of such a subsidy would require careful consideration.[23]

Still other methods of financing the postal system's fixed costs include establishing a special fund from the taxes paid by private delivery firms. Alternatively, the costs could be internalized within a subsidiary "delivery agency" that would be supported either by general tax revenues or by a special fund. The Postal Service could then serve exclusively as a collecting and sorting agency, turning the mails over to the subsidiary at the local post office of the addressee for ultimate delivery.

The point here is merely to emphasize that the basic issue over possible repeal of the letter monopoly is not whether it would lower costs or improve service. Clearly this would be the result for some elements of the business community that are heavy users of local letter-mail services. Rather, the basic issues are who would pay the increased costs for low-volume letter mail services, how those costs might be paid, and what the distributional effects of alternative financing solutions might be. Unfortunately, these are questions that even the economists who advocate repeal of the monopoly have left inadequately explored.

The questions, and their answers, remain largely academic in any event, since many factors make repeal of the postal monopoly very unlikely. First, Congress over the years has shaped a postal system that serves a wide array of social and political objectives: frequent delivery, maintenance of numerous collection and distribution points, continuation of a strong rural network, and universally available letter-mail service at reasonable and uniform rates. Repealing the monopoly would mean that some or all of these goals would have to be abandoned. The cost of this would be politically formidable, especially since the benefits of such a move are uncertain. Thus, the political consequences of repeal make it unattractive to elected officials, who would have to answer to the general mailing public.

Second, the political incentives for such a dramatic shift in public policy do not currently exist. Strong opposition would come from the postal unions that have become so expert in lobbying Congress. And the users of other classes of mail would fight the monopoly's repeal out of fear that their pocketbooks would be hurt, since certain losses in the volume of first-class mail would force higher rates on them. On the other side, there are no strong groups favoring the monopoly's repeal. Persons or groups who might benefit from such a change are probably not aware of it or do not have a strong enough incentive to organize to fight for its enactment.

Third, the Postal Service is already meeting two of the key objectives of those who advocate increased competition—innovation and responsiveness to market needs. For example, the Postal Service has developed a vigorous and successful guaranteed overnight package delivery service (Express Mail Service). The Postal Service also has responded to growing market demand for express delivery of letters by proposing to give up part of its letter monopoly to allow private carriers to deliver letters that have to be delivered very quickly.[24] In addition, the Postal Service has instituted rate discounts for pre-sorted first-class mail and second- and third-class mail that has been sorted by carrier route; the attractiveness of the postal system has thereby been improved, compared with alternative forms of delivery.

Finally, the Postal Service *already* faces substantial competitive pressures in its letter-mail market from electronic communications systems. We should understand the nature of that competition, the Postal Service's response to it, and the regulatory and political issues involved. These matters are important because the Postal Service's role in the telecommunications market is fast becoming a serious public policy issue.

Competition in the Communications Market

Over the past half-century, communications patterns in the United States have undergone marked changes. In 1930 the Post Office Department and the telephone system carried roughly the same number of messages. Since that time, the message volumes handled by both systems have increased substantially, but the postal system's share of the total message market has declined. The telephone industry now handles approximately 80 per cent of the nation's total exchange messages and the postal system only about 20 per cent.[25]

Today the Postal Service is facing new competitive challenges as imaginative communications applications of fast-changing electronic technologies appear poised to encroach significantly on the traditional market for first-class mail. Electronic Funds Transfer Systems (EFTS) and Electronic Message Transmission Systems (EMTS) are two developments that present an extraordinary challenge to the Postal Service. They have the ability together to meet most of the "mail" needs of the business community, which currently accounts for 80 per cent of the total volume of first-class mail with invoices, bills, statements of account, financial papers, business correspondence, and other business-related material. Because of the transmission and information-storage capacities of new electronic-communications technologies (including microprocessors mounted on silicon chips, glass fiber optics, broadband satellite connections, new visual-display instruments, and high-speed printers), it is *already* technologically possible to transmit more than 50 per cent of the current mailstream by electronic means. Consultants from Arthur D. Little, Inc., have estimated that as early as 1985 these technological capacities could be in such wide use as to divert some 17 billion, or 23 per cent, of the 73.5 billion pieces of first-class mail projected for that year.[26] As one observer of these new developments has suggested: "The outlook for the Postal Service is a rapidly changing market structure in which cream-skimming will occur on a grand scale. . . . The Postal Service can anticipate losing not merely the cream but virtually the entire dairy business to the new electronic competitors." [27] The Postal Service is already noticing the drain on its first-class-mail volume from all these electronic developments, and just now from EFTS in particular.

Electronic Funds Transfer Systems

Electronic systems for transferring funds encompass a broad range of possible systems for recording financial transactions. These involve substituting an electronic transfer of funds for conventional payment systems—in other words, substituting an electronic impulse for checks or cash. Significant diversions in the volume of first-class mail are expected from some EFTS-related developments.

For example, although the practice is not new, many consumers arrange to have fixed, recurring bills, such as life and health insurance premiums and home mortgage payments, automatically paid from their bank accounts. In the past, it was common practice for, say, an insurance company to mail banks regular statements debiting each payer's checking account. But it is now increasingly com-

mon for computers to transfer the funds electronically from one account to another through a special new network of facilities known
as automated clearinghouses (ACH). The resulting loss to the Postal
Service of first-class-mail volume is substantial, as the number of
monthly billings and payments of the policyholders of the nation's
insurance carriers alone can attest. In 1979 the Metropolitan Life
Insurance Company, for example, had about 560,000 of its pre-
authorized monthly premium collections handled electronically
through the ACH system.[28]

Another EFTS-related development that threatens the volume of
first-class mail is the growth of direct-deposit programs through
which large corporations and government agencies offer employees
or other payees the choice of having their regular payments depos-
ited directly in a bank. Instead of mailing out thousands of checks,
the employer either supplies financial institutions with lists or magnetic computer tapes indicating names and accounts to be credited
or clears the transactions through ACH. Particularly worrisome to
the Postal Service are the diversions in first-class mail resulting
from the direct-deposit programs of other government agencies. In
1974 the U.S. Treasury Department began depositing Social Security checks directly. It later expanded this practice to include retirement payments for railroad and civil service workers and the
U.S. Navy and Air Force and also Veterans Administration benefits.
The Treasury also plans to include in the future all payments under
the Army and Marine Corps retirement programs. As of July 1979,
the federal government's direct-deposit programs involved 10.3
million payments monthly. That number is likely to expand, since
only 24 per cent of federal-payment recipients eligible for this service are now participating, and both the Treasury Department and
financial institutions are vigorously promoting direct deposit.[29]

The Postal Service also stands to lose a substantial amount
(though as yet unestimated) of the first-class mail associated with
local retail department store billings. The electronic check-
verification systems already in place in many stores could easily be
transformed into so-called point-of-sale (POS) terminals, permitting
immediate electronic transfer of funds at the time of sale. Point-of-
sale terminals, although typically owned by commercial banks, are
placed at the checkout or service counters of retailers (department
stores and supermarkets, for example). Sales clerks operating the

POS terminals simply enter the customer's personal identification number and data relevant to the transaction (retailer's identification number, price, date, and so forth), making an immediate electronic transfer from the customer's bank account to the account of the retailer. Depending on consumer and retailer acceptance, such a system could eventually replace millions of pieces of first-class mail now generated through billings, deposits, and the like.[30]

Finally, in many cities, banks already provide customers with the opportunity for paying bills (utility, department store, and the like) or transferring funds between accounts over their telephones. Users of traditional rotary-dial telephones need the help of an operator at the bank. But customers with Touch-Tone® telephones simply use them as computer terminals, calling a special number at the bank, keying in an identification number and then, with the help of recorded instructions, entering other information needed to complete bill payments. Payments are electronically deducted from customer accounts and routed to the accounts of the parties being paid; it is all done without checks, and without postage. From the projected growth of telephone bill-paying services nationwide and from the transaction volumes handled by banks currently offering such services, the Postal Service in 1979 estimated that telephone payment systems could mean the loss of anywhere from 625 million to 2.5 billion pieces of first-class mail each year, depending on consumer acceptance of the new systems.[31]

All these developments, contributing to what is now being called the checkless society, cause postal officials great anxiety. The implications for the diversion of first-class mail come into sharp relief when one considers the potential number of pieces of mail associated with a traditional check payment: (1) the bill or invoice sent by the firm requiring payment; (2) the mailing of the check from the payer to the recipient; (3) the mailing of the check by the recipient to the bank for deposit; and (4) the various mailings from the bank such as receipts, notices, and new mail-deposit envelopes.[32] The loss of all these and other mailings from the mailstream is a weighty concern to the Postal Service, given estimates that by 1985 about 6.2 billion pieces of first-class mail may be diverted annually because of EFTS-related developments, and the potential for substantially greater diversion.[33]

Electronic Message Transmission Systems

Paralleling the clear threat to the Postal Service's first-class mail revenues from EFTS is the rapid development of new telecommunications technologies and electronic transmission systems. These advances promise to lower the cost of communications and in the process, sharply alter the place of the Postal Service in the nation's communicating habits. There are new developments in integrated circuitry, including microprocessors that enable enormous reductions in the costs of message storage and retrieval. In systems for transmitting information, we now have communications satellites, fiber optics, and enhanced coaxial cables. All these foundation stones of new telecommunications systems go far beyond the traditional telephone or even the now-familiar TWX/Telex systems provided by Western Union. Along with new, low-cost video display terminals, software packages, and high-speed printers, these developments are contributing to revolutionary changes in the business world's communications systems and may together spell the end of traditional document-delivery services such as the postal system.[34]

The communications services based on these technological inventions are many and varied. The systems generally considered to have the greatest potential for being a direct substitute for first-class mail are facsimile systems—machines that function much like ordinary office copying machines but scan a document and transmit it electronically to a receiving terminal, where it is reproduced exactly.

Facsimile systems are not new nor is their threat to the postal stream a new fear to postal officials. As long ago as 1872, Postmaster General Jonathan Creswell noted in the Post Office Department's annual report:[35]

> *The probable simplification of the facsimile system of Caselli, by which an exact copy of anything that can be drawn or written may be instantaneously made to appear at a distance of hundreds of miles from the original; and the countless other applications of electricity to the transmission of intelligence yet to be made—must sooner or later interfere most seriously with the transportation of letters by the slower means of the post.*

The technology has existed for some time. But as with many telecommunications systems, the problem has been in making the technology economically feasible and developing a market for it. In the past decade or so, communications and business-machine companies have refined both the technology and the economics of facsimile systems. The new facsimile systems now manufactured and marketed largely by Xerox, Exxon, and the 3M Company are able to transmit higher-quality reproductions in seconds; they are using the new digital scanning equipment and lower-priced transmission methods—not just telephone lines but microwave relays and satellites. All these developments are contributing to rapid acceleration in the number of facsimile units in use by businesses throughout the United States. There were over 200,000 facsimile units in place in 1980, and one study estimates that there will be nearly 500,000 in place by 1985, transmitting an approximate total of 5.5 billion messages per year.[36]

Other communications developments similarly threatening the first-class mailstream stem from many improvements over the past decade in microprocessors and integrated circuits. Today's silicon chips store over 60,000 bits of information. By 1985, chips will be available that store one million bits, and computer scientists believe that they will eventually be able to store up to 30 million bits of information on a single chip smaller than a fingernail.[37] This fast-changing data-storage technology is reducing costs, with resulting revolutionary developments in business communications systems. The so-called store-and-forward systems are an example. The sender, using his own terminal, enters messages or data, which are then stored in the memory of a computer at a remote location. Then the receiver, at his convenience, connects with the computer via his own terminal and draws off the information onto either a printer or a video display screen. "Communicating Word Processors" (CWPs) are a type of store-and-forward system now being used by Sears, Citicorp, General Electric, and other large corporations, primarily for intracompany communications. The operator of a CWP can type in the figures of a table or type in the text of a document (editing right on the display screen if necessary) and then order the document transmitted to a single recipient or to many at a cost (in 1979) of 60 to 70 cents a transmission—substantially less than the current cost a business office incurs in the typing, correcting, filing, and mailing of a single paper document.[38]

With all these and other developing telecommunications technologies, the threat to first-class-mail volume is extraordinary. A study Arthur D. Little, Inc., prepared in 1978 for the Commission

on Postal Service estimated that in 1985, *non-EFTS* electronic communications could divert as much as 8.6 billion pieces of first-class
mail annually from the Postal Service.[39] All such estimates are spec-
ulative, but the point remains the same, that electronic communications systems pose a substantial threat (in the billions of pieces) to
postal volumes and revenues.

Though there does not seem to be much the Postal Service can
do about the revenue and volume diversions caused by EFTS, the
Service has sought to develop abilities of its own in transmitting
electronic messages. These initiatives have engendered controversy,
as we shall now see.

Endnotes

1. U.S., Postal Service, Customer Services Department, Marketing Services Division, "Competitors and Competition of the U.S. Postal Service," vol. 13 (November 1979), mimeographed, p. 18.
2. *Ibid.*, p. 15. Also see *Business Week*, July 18, 1970, p. 95.
3. Postal Service, "Competitors and Competition," vol. 13, p. 23.
4. Comptroller General of the United States, *Grim Outlook for the United States
   Postal Service's National Bulk Mail System*, report to the Congress (Washington: General Accounting Office, May 16, 1978), #GGD-78-59, pp. 12, 14, 15.
5. *Ibid.*, p. 9.
6. *Business Week*, July 18, 1970, p. 94.
7. John Haldi, *Postal Monopoly: An Assessment of the Private Express Statutes*
   (Washington: American Enterprise Institute, 1974), pp. 23–25.
8. U.S., Congress, House, Committee on Post Office and Civil Service, *Postal
   Service Staff Study: "Necessity for Change,"* Committee Print No. 94-26, 94th
   Cong., 2d Sess., 1976, p. 29.
9. Postal Service, "Competitors and Competition of the U.S. Postal Service," vol.
   13, pp. 4, 9.
10. *U.S. News and World Report*, March 22, 1976, p. 25.
11. See testimony in U.S., Congress, House, Committee on Post Office and Civil
    Service, *Private Express Statutes, hearings before a Subcommittee of the Com-
    mittee on Post Office and Civil Service*, 96th Cong., 1st Sess., 1979, Serial No.
    96-39, p. 81.
12. Postal Service, "Competitors and Competition of the U.S. Postal Service," vol.
    13, p. 7.
13. *National Association of Letter Carriers v. Independent Postal System of Amer-
    ica, Inc.*, 336 F. Supp. 804 (W.D. Okla 1971), aff'd 470 F. 2d 265 (10th cir.,
    1972).
14. See *New York Times*, August 6, 1978, p. 41; and *Washington Post*, July 30,
    1978, p. A4.

15. See, for example, John Haldi, *Postal Monopoly: An Assessment of the Private Express Statutes* (Washington: American Enterprise Institute, 1974); Milton Friedman, "The Post Office," *Newsweek*, October 9, 1967, p. 87.

16. Haldi, *Postal Monopoly*, p. 34.

17. *Ibid.*, pp. 37–38.

18. McKinsey and Company, Inc., "Cream Skimming: The Threat of Private Sector Competition for First-Class Mail," in U.S., Congress, House, Committee on Post Office and Civil Service, *Statutes Restricting Private Carriage of Mail and Their Administration*, Committee Print No. 93-5, 93rd Cong., 1st Sess., 1973, p. 120.

19. *Postal Service Staff Study, "Necessity for Change,"* House Committee Print No. 94-26, p. 28.

20. Commission on Postal Service, *Report of the Commission on Postal Service* (Washington: U.S. Government Printing Office, 1977), vol. 2, pp. 700–701.

21. *Ibid.*, pp. 774–775.

22. *Ibid.*, p. 776.

23. *Ibid.*, pp. 776–777.

24. See *Washington Post*, July 10, 1979, p. D10; also *Federal Register*, 44, no. 132, July 9, 1979, 40076.

25. Donald R. Ewing and Roger K. Salaman, "The Postal Crisis: The Postal Function as a Communications Service," U.S. Department of Commerce, Office of Telecommunications Special Publication 77-13, January 1977, p. 3.

26. *Report of the Commission on Postal Service*, vol. 1, pp. 19–20.

27. Bridger M. Mitchell, "Commentary," in Roger Sherman, ed., *Perspectives on Postal Service Issues* (Washington: American Enterprise Institute, 1980), p. 133.

28. Postal Service, "Competitors and Competition," vol. 13, p. 50.

29. *Ibid.*, pp. 50–51.

30. Henry Geller and Stuart Brotman, "Electronic Alternatives to Postal Service," in Glen O. Robinson, ed., *Communications for Tomorrow* (New York: Praeger Publishers, 1978), p. 323.

31. Postal Service, "Competitors and Competition," vol. 13, p. 52.

32. *Report of the Commission on Postal Service*, vol. 1, p. 22.

33. *Ibid.*, vol. 2, p. 574.

34. See Geller and Brotman, "Electronic Alternatives," esp. pp. 314–322.

35. U.S., Post Office Department, *Annual Report of the Postmaster General, 1872*, p. 30; quoted in John F. McLaughlin, "Electronic Mail: Defining a Role for the U.S. Postal Service," remarks at Fourth Annual Telecommunications Policy Research Conference, Airlie, Va., April 1976, pp. 4–5.

36. *Report of the Commission on Postal Service*, vol. 2, p. 503.

37. See *Washington Post*, June 4, 1980, p. A5.

38. Postal Service, "Competitors and Competition of the U.S. Postal Service," vol. 13, p. 40.

39. *Report of the Commission on Postal Service*, vol. 2, p. 574.

Chapter 8

THE POSTAL SERVICE AND ELECTRONIC COMMUNICATIONS

Few tasks facing postal executives in the 1970s have been more important than developing an organizational response to technological changes in communications. Since the rapid rise of electronic message transmission systems presages an end to the days of the traditional delivery of documents, it is no surprise to find the Postal Service advancing its own electronic message services in an effort to stave off organizational decline. These initiatives by the Postal Service have provoked predictable controversies about the propriety of governmental involvement in this field and about how much the Postal Service should be involved in electronic transmission. Not the least of the obstacles the Postal Service has met in launching its new services are the regulatory hurdles constructed by the Postal Rate Commission.

Early Electronic Services

The Postal Service has tentatively ventured into electronic communications at various times in recent decades. The old Post Office Department in 1959 tested "Speed Mail," a domestic facsimile experiment between Washington and Chicago using facilities supplied by private carriers. But J. Edward Day, President Kennedy's postmaster general, ended the experiment early in 1961 in response

155

to protests by Western Union and to the concerns of some within the postal establishment that scarce research and development funds should be concentrated on improving the conventional mail services.[1]

The first significant step by the Postal Service into the electronic age came soon after the agency's reorganization. In a move touched by irony, the Postal Service announced in 1971 the start of a joint venture with Western Union to provide a message service (now familiar as "Mailgram") that would be cheaper than a conventional telegram but faster than a normal letter. Mailgram messages are transmitted electronically over Western Union's communications network to selected post offices for delivery by regular letter carriers in the next business day's mail. (Mailgram is primarily a store-and-forward system. The sender enters the message via Telex/ TWX, computer, telephone, or delivery to a Western Union office or to Western Union's computer facility in Middletown, Virginia. The receiving post office draws the message off a teleprinter, inserts it in an envelope, and delivers it through first-class mail.) The Mailgram service has been successful from its inception; volume has soared from 1.2 million Mailgrams in 1971 to 37.6 million in 1979.[2]

Though the Postal Service's other advances in the electronic communications field have been slow in coming, they have been considerably more ambitious and not surprisingly have raised many issues and engendered much political controversy. Under the determined leadership of Postmaster General William Bolger, who took office in March 1978, the Postal Service has moved forward with three new service proposals. These are INTELPOST (International Electronic Post), EMS (Electronic Message Service System), and E-COM (Electronic Computer Originated Mail).

INTELPOST and EMS

In March 1978, the Postal Service announced a plan to test a system for high-speed overseas satellite transmission of facsimile copies; this would be a joint venture with the Communications Satellite Corporation. The Postal Service awarded a contract in 1978 to ITT World Communications to install and maintain the international communications links for the test program. The contract called for ITT to set up channels for transmitting facsimiles by satellites between the United States and seven countries: Argentina, Belgium, West Germany, France, Iran, the Netherlands, and the United Kingdom. Receiving countries would use their traditional mail-delivery systems to provide one-day delivery (same-day delivery if transmitted before noon) of the instantaneously transmitted copies. The cost to customers would be $5 a page.[3]

The Postal Service started testing INTELPOST in July 1979, transmitting between the United States and London. But before it could begin a one-year trial service of its connections to the other six countries, a regulatory setback took place. On October 18, 1979, the chief of the Common Carrier Bureau of the Federal Communications Commission refused in an administrative decision to grant permission to two satellite carriers with trans-Atlantic links to lease their services to the Postal Service. Rejecting the bids of RCA Global Communications and TRT Telecommunications Corporation, the FCC characterized the service as "inherently discriminatory," insofar as these two carriers normally did not lease their circuits for resale to others. As this is written, the Postal Service is still deciding its next step on INTELPOST. It may appeal the decision to the FCC commissioners or possibly to the federal courts.[4]

Meanwhile the Postal Sevice, convinced that recent inventions have made full-scale, nationwide facsimile systems economically feasible, has been pushing ahead with plans for such a system; it is the Electronic Message Service System (EMS). The Radio Corporation of America (RCA), under contract to the Postal Service, helped design a nationwide facsimile system that would involve 87 cities, cost $1.7 billion, and be ready by 1990. At its research and development laboratories in Rockville, Maryland, the Postal Service in 1979 tested a $675,000 prototype scanner capable of converting documents into electronic impulses at the rate of 10 pages a second. The scanner would be connected to a $2.5 million printing and paper-handling system (developed for the Postal Service by Pitney Bowes Corp.) that converts the electronic impulses back into print, and folds and inserts the pages into addressed envelopes at the rate of 4 pages a second.[5] A study by RCA estimated that with sufficient volume, EMS services in the decade from 1985 to 1995 could be provided at a cost to customers of 10 or 11 cents a message—considerably less than the 15 cents the Postal Service charged in 1980 for a first-class letter.[6] The Postal Service plans to introduce a 10-city test phase of this program in 1984.

Electronic Computer Originated Mail (E-COM)

The plans for INTELPOST and EMS (both facsimile systems), though ambitious and controversial, have yet to generate as much policy debate as E-COM, the Postal Service's boldest step into the electronic age. Postmaster General Bolger announced in August 1978 that the Postal Service planned to offer business mailers a new service for electronically transmitting computer-generated messages—principally bills, dunning notices, uniform correspondence, and the like—directly to local post offices, where they will be printed out on high-speed printing equipment, automatically enclosed in envelopes, and distributed in the traditional way by letter carriers. The Postal Service will lease the transmission services— microwave towers, radio, and satellite—from telecommunications common carriers. Approximately 750 companies, including banks, insurance companies, and public utilities, have been identified by the Postal Service as likely users of the service. Rates for the new service, which goes into effect on January 4, 1982, will initially be 30 cents for the first printed page and 10 cents for the second. The Postal Service expects that E-COM could eventually unfold into a service conveying 15.6 billion pieces of computer-generated mail annually.[7]

Controversies over Postal Service Entry

The Postal Service's entry into the electronic communications field has received predictably strong opposition from the communications lobby. These opponents are the big telecommunications companies (especially Xerox, AT&T, Exxon, IBM, ITT, and 3M, and newer competitors such as Graphnet Systems, Inc., and Telenet Corp.) and the Communications Workers of America (AFL-CIO). Unfavorably disposed also are assorted officials in Congress and in the executive branch, particularly in the National Telecommunications Information Administration (NTIA), the agency charged with long-range telecommunications planning. These and other opponents have advanced many reasons for barring Postal Service entry into electronic mail. Some of this opposition is based on what Kenneth Robinson has called "residual prejudices to any expansion in government enterprise," and on the belief that large public utilities should be kept in their proper place and not be permitted to diversify. Robinson explains:[8]

Much of the literature suggests that expansive government enterprise contributes to the erosion of the entrepreneurial spirit, socialism, and other presumed ills. Less doctrinal objections include the fact that government enterprises result in taxes forgone, contribute to more of our gross national product filtering through a public bureaucracy, result in confused signals to the private sector and investors, and the like.

More to the point, opponents of Postal Service entry into the electronic message market argue that this is not, after all, a field in which the nation is now lacking full or improving services. On the contrary, as Henry Geller, the head of the National Telecommunications Information Administration (an agency clearly not friendly to the Postal Service initiatives), has indicated: "With the pro-competition policies being pursued by the FCC, the field is filled with new entrants pushing the emerging technology and services as rapidly as possible." [9]

In addition, the communications lobby and its friends argue that the Postal Service is crying wolf—that it is by no means clear that the postal system would lose business even if it is prevented from entering the electronic transmission field. Officials in the NTIA have even insisted that there might be an increase in the volume of first-class mail regardless of whether the Postal Service itself offers electronic services. This argument has it that until homes are universally equipped with message receivers (foreseeable, but still some time off), the Postal Service will end up delivering copies of electronically generated messages, since no private carriers would be able to duplicate the postal system's relatively efficient delivery network.[10]

Arguing in favor of Postal Service entry into the electronic communications field are the various elements of the postal lobby—the Postal Service itself, the unions representing its 650,000 employees, some members of Congress, and many businesses that use the mails heavily. As in the case of the opponents' arguments, there is an undeniably strong element of self-protection in the arguments of most of those who support Postal Service entry. The postal lobby, realizing that the postal system is sure to lose billions of pieces of mail in coming years (even if only from EFTS diversions), is worried that the cycle of cumulative deterioration of postal volumes and revenues will accelerate. Urban Lehner of the *Wall Street Journal* has summarized the basic premise behind the postal lobby's support for electronic mail services as follows. The postal system will continue to be needed (at least for the foreseeable future) to deliver items that people cannot or will not want to send electronically (catalogues and love letters, for example). That delivery system entails fixed costs, which must be paid regardless of the volume (the letter carrier makes his appointed rounds whether he delivers ten items or only one to each house). Thus, the Postal Service faces the same dilemma here that it would face if the private express statutes were repealed. If billions of pieces of mail are diverted from the postal system, the Postal Service will have to raise rates for the remaining mail to meet its fixed costs. Increased rates would lead to still greater volume diversions, and thus eventually to the extinction of the Postal Service or to exorbitant rates for the remaining customers. Such an eventuality is naturally unacceptable to postal officials, to the legions of postal employees, and to those who will continue to rely on the conventional mail system's delivery apparatus. These groups believe that the Postal Service has to begin offering a variety of electronic message services to businesses and individuals to ensure the organization's survival in an electronic age. Postmaster General Bolger has articulated the stark challenge facing his organization: "Our choice is to attempt to adapt to electronic communications or eventually be overwhelmed by it." [11]

In a less self-protective line of argument, the postal lobby has argued that if electronic communications services are to be available to everyone, the government must get involved since private firms will simply skim the cream, concentrating on only the most lucrative kinds of high-volume, business-to-business service, leaving a telecommunications gap in the most difficult and costly area of service, that to the home (either business-to-home or home-to-home). There is an unserved market here, one the government can serve without incurring charges of stifling private inventiveness, and one that the Postal Service has a positive mandate to serve under its charter to provide nationwide household delivery.

Moreover, the Postal Reorganization Act included several explicit provisions clearly intended to ensure that the Postal Service would have both the responsibility and the authority to use developing technologies to improve service and control costs. The act requires that the Postal Service should:[12]

1. Provide prompt, reliable, and efficient services to patrons.
2. Give the highest consideration to the requirement for the most expeditious collection, transportation, and delivery of important letter mail.
3. Receive, transmit, and deliver written and printed matter and provide such other services incidental thereto as it finds appropriate to its functions and in the public interest.
4. Provide for the collection, handling, transportation, delivery, forwarding, returning, and holding of mail.
5. Provide, establish, change, or abolish special nonpostal or similar services.
6. Promote modern and efficient operations and refrain from engaging in any practice that restricts the use of new equipment or devices that may reduce the cost or improve the quality of postal services.
7. Have all other powers incidental, necessary, or appropriate to carrying on its functions or the exercise of its specific powers.

The legislative history of the Postal Reorganization Act also shows that Congress was particularly concerned with enabling the postal system to keep its services up to date in a rapidly changing age. In the words of a House committee, the postal reorganization legislation sought to establish "a national postal service that is forever searching for new markets and new ways by which the communications needs of the American people may be served." [13] In this vein, the Postal Service sees electronic mail as simply the latest in a long history of new developments adopted by the organization in performing its mission of public service. One postal official observed, "We don't look on it any differently than moving from stage coach to a train to a jet plane." [14]

Whatever the merits of the arguments over such a move, there is no longer any doubt that the Postal Service will enter the electronic communications field. The Postal Service appears to have clear statutory authority to take such steps, and it also has formidable political support for its actions. The large and powerful postal unions solidly support the Service's electronic diversification, and so do the bulk of business mailers. Moreover, in 1979 the Carter Administration issued a strong endorsement of electronic mail, encouraging the Postal Service to compete, within certain restrictions, in the transmission of telecommunications messages.[15] There are also significant congressional pressures urging postal management to act to save the mail system from its cycle of cumulative deterioration. Finally, not many prominent politicians are arguing strongly against permitting the Postal Service to improve the speed and quality of mail services by adopting refined electronic technologies.[16]

Since there are so many supporting considerations and the effective opposition is relatively small, the Postal Service has confidently committed itself to providing various forms of electronic mail service; and there seems little prospect that its moves will be reversed now. Thus, the debate about whether the Postal Service should enter the electronic field is now essentially moot. Important policy issues remain, however, such as how wide a range of electronic services the Postal Service should be permitted to provide.

Limiting the Postal Service Role

One of the principal concerns of the communications lobby is that the Postal Service will not limit its entry to its current plans, which involve so-called Generation II services. (By this method, both the input and the transmission of messages are electronic, but the output is hard copy ready for hand delivery by the USPS.) The concern is that the Postal Service, in an effort to ensure its survival into the 21st century, will use these services to establish its footing in the electronic market. Opponents insist that then, when post offices and letter carriers have been rendered nearly obsolete by the development of affordable facsimile receivers for use in homes, the Postal Service will expand into systems that are fully electronic from sender to receiver (so-called Generation III). Stanford Weinstein, an attorney for Graphnet Systems, Inc. (one of the chief new entrants in the electronic message market), expressed what is worrying the communications industry:[17]

> Ten years from now, when lots of businesses and even homes have their own black boxes, the Postal Service is going to be saying, "Gee, we could make a lot more money on this if we were in Generation III." And at that point, from a policy standpoint, it will make little logical sense to keep them out. If they're receiving messages electronically, for delivery to someone who has the capability to receive electronically, why should they have to deliver the message to them by hand?

The Postal Service, for its part, denies any current intention to move toward electronic transmission of facsimile printouts directly to home or business terminals. The Postal Service argues that its strength lies in its unmatched delivery network, for which there will always be a need, and further that its purpose in instituting electronic service is to control labor and transportation costs, keep rates down, and improve the speed of its services.

In spite of these solemn assurances from the Postal Service, the communications lobby would like to see adoption of public policies ensuring that the provision of Generation III services will be explicitly reserved to private carriers. Other observers see no reason why the Postal Service should be excluded from providing *fully* electronic services if the technology changes, making home terminals practical. Kenneth Robinson, a communications lawyer in the Antitrust Division of the U.S. Department of Justice, has argued, for example:[18]

> *Presumably any decision to permit the Postal Service to enter electronic communications would reflect the judgment that this major institution should be allowed to make use of new technologies and should be permitted to participate in a field as its current line of business is eroded. A further presumption is that we should not adopt the so-called Curtis LeMay approach of relegating the Postal Service to what is, by comparison with new electronic services, a Stone Age technology. If the Postal Service does in fact enter electronic mail services to any significant extent, it seems to make little sense to endeavor to hedge that technology with standards and classifications that may themselves be shortly overcome by subsequent technological advances.*

Whatever the range of electronic mail services the Postal Service eventually offers, it will face clear limitations on its autonomy. It will not have sole jurisdiction over the electronic transmission of messages, since new and existing telecommunications firms clearly will provide brisk competition and acquire substantial market shares. The nature of Postal Service electronic offerings, moreover, will be subject to policy decisions by Congress and by federal regulatory agencies. Both the Postal Rate Commission and the Federal Communications Commission have staked some claim to regulatory jurisdiction over electronic mail. Whichever agency ultimately prevails, the Postal Service's E-COM service has already been shaped substantially by the activities of the regulators.

The E-COM Proposal and Regulatory Tangles

The Federal Communications Commission (FCC) was drawn into the fray over E-COM in November 1978, when Graphnet Systems Inc. filed with the FCC a request for a declaratory ruling and clarification on the regulatory status of the FCC with respect to E-COM. In response to Graphnet's petition, the FCC issued what is known as a Memorandum Opinion and Order, in which the commission asserted regulatory jurisdiction over the Postal Service's entire E-COM service. The FCC, noting the pro-competition policies reflected in its recent decisions, claimed it has statutory responsibility to make certain that no telecommunications services offered by the Postal Service have the effect of lessening competition or discouraging investment in private telecommunications carriers.[19] As originally designed, the E-COM proposal called for the Postal Service to lease electronic transmission services (microwave and satellite) exclusively from Western Union and then let businesses hook into them to send computer-generated messages to local post offices. The FCC's Common Carrier Bureau had earlier rejected Western Union's application for authority to provide the electronic links in the proposed E-COM system, saying that the system as planned was non-competitive and discriminatory.[20] The commission apparently was concerned that competition would be stifled if no other telecommunications companies besides Western Union were permitted to link with the system. The Postal Service later filed a suit in the U.S. Court of Appeals in Washington, challenging the FCC's claim of regulatory jurisdiction over the E-COM service.[21]

Meanwhile, the Postal Rate Commission (PRC) had become involved with E-COM when the Postal Service, as required by law, filed a proposal with the PRC to offer E-COM as an electronic mail subclass. Just as in its rate and classification cases, the PRC conducted formal hearings on the E-COM proposal, entertaining the arguments of the Postal Service, of mail users who had chosen to participate as intervenors, and of the Officer of the Commission (OOC), who (as noted in Chapter 6) is required by law to "represent the interests of the general public."

The OOC favored an "alternative design" for E-COM, with the aim of encouraging more competition in the electronic transmission part of the service than what would have existed under the exclusive arrangement the Postal Service had proposed with Western Union. Under the OOC's proposal, any communications common carrier that could gain approval from the FCC would be allowed to receive and transmit electronic messages directly to those post offices specially equipped to handle E-COM services. The OOC's plan was based on the argument that cost savings and service improvements would result from having several companies competing for the electronic transmission segment of the service. Calculations presented by the PRC suggested that under the OOC's plan, customers would incur a cost of only about 27 cents a message instead of the 42 cents a message likely under the Postal Service's plan.[22]

On December 17, 1979, the PRC, adopting the OOC's proposal, issued its recommended decision (by a 3 to 2 vote), saying the Postal Service could offer its E-COM service, but requiring that the Postal Service allow other qualified telecommunications carriers to interconnect with the system rather than Western Union alone. The PRC found the "decentralized" model of the OOC superior to the Postal Service's plan for two reasons. Not only did it promise technically superior service at a lower cost and foster competition in telecommunications (being thus consistent with FCC efforts and with policy pronouncements of the Carter Administration), but it seemed to offer a way of keeping the Postal Service outside the jurisdiction of the FCC.[23]

The Postal Service Board of Governors accepted the "basic premises" of the PRC's recommended decision, that there should be "full and free competition for the electronic transmission portions of the system with access to the postal delivery network available to all on a nondiscriminatory basis." But the postal governors were unhappy with the PRC's decision for several reasons. Most important, they felt that the PRC's decision was not clear enough on several key matters relating to the Postal Service's authority over E-COM. These ambiguities included whether the Postal Service could, under certain circumstances (such as insufficient participation by private firms), contract directly with telecommunications carriers to transmit E-COM messages; whether mailers would be permitted to establish direct connections between their own telecommunications systems and post offices, rather than use common carriers; and whether mailers would be permitted to bring magnetic computer tapes directly to post offices rather than send the data to post offices electronically. The postal governors also wanted the rate commission's decision to include language permitting the Postal Service to require assurances of performance (service quality, direction, and scope) from the telecommunications carriers participating in the service. Finally, the postal governors were displeased that the PRC had approved the E-COM service for only a limited time period. The governors argued that the imposition of a terminal date might "seriously impair the chances of ultimate success" for E-COM; moreover, they argued that the PRC lacked statutory authority to impose such a time limit. Because of all these concerns, the Postal Service Board of Governors on February 22, 1980, unanimously rejected the PRC's recommended decision and sent it back to the commission with a request for clarifications and modifications on these points.[24]

When the PRC issued its "further recommended decision" on April 8, 1980, it left some of these matters (the physical delivery of magnetic tapes and mailers' direct communications linkage to post offices) open for determination after further hearings. But the PRC granted the Postal Service the most important of the favorable clarifications the governors had wanted—that the Postal Service could, "on the basis of demonstrated need," contract directly with telecommunications firms to provide its own transmission of E-COM messages even if it would thus be competing with common carriers who had won FCC approval to transmit mail to post offices. This grant of permission by the PRC seemed likely to cause new regulatory problems, bringing the Postal Service back within the reach of the FCC. But recognizing that the Postal Service had gone to federal appeals court challenging the FCC's assertion of jurisdiction over electronic mail plans, the PRC left it to the Postal Service to work out those conflicts on its own. On the other hand, the PRC refused to grant the governors' request that the Postal Service be authorized to require "assurances of service quality, duration, and scope" from the telecommunications carriers that might link into the E-COM system. The PRC refused on the gounds that establishing performance or quality standards for carriers is tantamount to regulating them, and that authority already clearly belongs to the FCC.[25]

The PRC also refused to accede to the governors' request that E-COM be approved as a permanent service rather than on the "experimental" basis granted by the PRC with a termination date of

October 1, 1983. The PRC agreed only to postpone the terminal deadline a year. The reason is understandable; the temporary approval keeps the ball in the PRC's court and gives the commission substantial continuing power in the matter. It means that the E-COM service will automatically stop on October 1, 1984, unless the PRC issues a decision recommending that the service continue. If the PRC had granted permanent approval to E-COM, the commission would not have been in as strong a position to shape E-COM's development, since the Postal Service Board of Governors could simply reject any recommendation the commission might make.[26]

When the Postal Service announced in August 1980 that its E-COM service would commence on January 4, 1982, it also announced that it intended to sue the Postal Rate Commission in the U.S. Court of Appeals to reverse the PRC's decision to grant only temporary approval for E-COM. The postal Board of Governors asserted that the rate commission action went "far outside the commission's statutory authority." [27]

Thus, even as the Postal Service prepares for its first sizable electronic mail program, some basic questions remain unsettled. Questions over the appropriate regulatory roles of the FCC and the PRC relative to electronic mail are likely to persist, regardless of what decision the U.S. Court of Appeals eventually reaches. In the short run, however, the Postal Rate Commission has shown that it will not be content to play second fiddle to the FCC in this area. As one observer has noted:[28]

> *The PRC's seizure of the lead role in this matter has come as a surprise to most observers; and a shock to the Postal Service. An agency whose only explicit authority is to prevent mail rate and classification changes and post office closings has ended up drawing the jurisdictional demarcation between postal regulation and telecommunications regulation, assessing the relative advantages of open competition, and evaluating the technological and commercial feasibility of such electronic esoterica as multiplexing and archiving.*

The effective assertion by the PRC of control in this area is less surprising when one considers that the rate commission has nearly ten years' experience focusing its attention only on the activities of the Postal Service, whereas the FCC's assorted regulatory efforts are much more diffuse, covering the activities of dozens of large corporations. Another important factor is that unlike the PRC, the FCC is not accustomed to trying to regulate the activities of another government agency—a different matter altogether from dealing with even the most combative of private companies.[29]

Still, the FCC should not be counted out of this arena since it must approve E-COM's common carriers. Moreover, the controversies over regulatory issues are likely to intensify if the Postal Service continues to diversify its telecommunications offerings. The disagreements will become sharpest if the Postal Service ever moves toward extending its electronic services directly to home terminals. But decisions over a move of that import presumably would not be left in the hands of regulatory agencies; they probably would be made in Congress only after full deliberation and debate.

Postal Management: Ready for the Task?

The most interesting and important question is whether the current management structure of the Postal Service (which is well designed to provide layers of supervision over the labor-intensive operations of moving material) will be able to carry out the electronic mail services successfully. There is a popular tendency to view the Postal Service (not alone among government enterprises) as a bumbling and ill-managed outfit. But there is in fact little reason to believe that postal management will not be up to the task. In the past, the postal organization has successfully adapted its operations to technological changes, including the railroad and the airplane. Moreover, the new electronic service plans will circumvent the most difficult postal operation (sorting and transporting) and will capitalize, at least for a while, on the postal system's greatest strength, which is its delivery capacity. In addition, private telecommunications companies joining in the Postal Service's electronic mail ventures will have powerful financial incentives to help iron out problems and make the services attractive and mutually profitable. All this is not to say that the Postal Service faces no difficulties in its new services; rather, there is little *a priori* reason to predict failure.

The only cause for skepticism (and it is admittedly serious) is that the Postal Service continues to devote altogether too few resources to research and development. The Service has raised the symbolic importance of R&D by elevating its organizational status from a department to a management group, headed by a senior assistant postmaster general. Yet of the Postal Service's total operating expenses of $17.5 billion for fiscal 1979, a mere $15.7 million went to research and development—less than one tenth of 1 per cent.[30] This effort puts the Postal Service at the bottom of big American industries in research spending—even behind some industries that are not renowned for their own R&D efforts, such as textiles, wood products, and primary metals.[31] Even though the Postal Service will be relying on well-established private carriers for transmission, it is difficult to see how the new electronic message systems can be successful in the long run unless the Postal Service substantially increases its own research.

Future judgments about the success of the Postal Service's new electronic initiatives will likely be based on two kinds of data. These will indicate whether the services are commercially attractive (that is, whether they seem to be drawing enough of the market share to provide the postal system with sustaining volumes), and whether they have enabled the Postal Service substantially to reduce labor costs as a percentage of total costs. Eventually, of course, judgment will rest on whether these initiatives enabled the Postal Service to survive.

Whatever those future judgments, the electronic initiatives themselves can be seen as an indication that postal executives, particularly since William Bolger became postmaster general, are thinking through the questions that Peter Drucker says are critical to good business management: "What is our business, and what should it be?" [32] Today, the Postal Service's answers are no longer exclusively tied to the physical movement of materials from point X to point Y. The Postal Service now also defines its business as communicating information. That, after all, is what is valuable to the consumers of its services. That management decision may well be the most important one in the postal system's history if it ensures the survival of the organization.

Endnotes

1. See *New York Times*, March 29, 1978, p. 52.
2. U.S. Postal Service, *Annual Report of the Postmaster General, 1971–1972*, p. 12; and U.S. Postal Service, "Comprehensive Statement on Postal Operations" (January 1980), p. 19.
3. Lawrence Mosher, "Policy Disputes Are Stalling Plans for Moving Mail Electronically," *National Journal*, November 3, 1979, p. 1841.

4. See *New York Times*, October 19, 1979, p. A14; also Mosher, "Policy Disputes," p. 1841.
5. Mosher, "Policy Disputes," p. 1841.
6. *New York Times*, November 22, 1978, p. A8.
7. *New York Times*, April 7, 1979, p. 29.
8. Kenneth Robinson, "The Postal Service and Electronic Communications: Various Legal Issues and Sundry Open Questions," in Roger Sherman, ed., *Perspectives on Postal Service Issues* (Washington: American Enterprise Institute, 1980), p. 168.
9. Henry Geller and Stuart Brotman, "Electronic Alternatives to Postal Service," in Glen O. Robinson, ed., *Communications for Tomorrow* (New York: Praeger Publishers, 1978), p. 333.
10. Urban C. Lehner, "Postal Service Vies with Private Concerns to Lead Entry into Electronic-Mail Age," *Wall Street Journal*, July 17, 1979, p. 46.
11. Quoted in Lehner, *ibid.* Reprinted by permission of *The Wall Street Journal*, © Dow Jones & Company, Inc., 1979. All rights reserved.
12. The specific sections of the Postal Reorganization Act of 1970 containing these requirements are (in the order presented in the text) *United States Code*, Title 39, sec. 101(a); sec. 101(e); sec. 403(a); sec. 404(1); sec. 404(6); sec. 2010; sec 401(10).
13. U.S., Congress, House, Committee on Post Office and Civil Service, *Postal Reorganization and Salary Adjustment Act of 1970*, H.Rept. No. 91-1104, to accompany H.R. 17070, 91st Cong., 2d Sess., 1970, p. 20.
14. James V. P. Conway, senior assistant postmaster general, quoted in *New York Times*, May 27, 1979, p. 33.
15. *New York Times*, July 20, 1979, p. D2; and *Washington Post*, July 20, 1979, p. E1.
16. Mosher, "Policy Disputes," p. 1843.
17. Quoted in Lehner, "Postal Service Vies with Private Concerns," p. 46. Reprinted by permission of *The Wall Street Journal*, © Dow Jones & Company, Inc., 1979. All rights reserved.
18. Robinson, "Postal Service and Electronic Communications," p. 175.
19. Graphnet Systems, Inc., 73 F.C.C. 2d 283, 296, 300 (1979).
20. Western Union Telegraph Co., Tariff F.C.C. No. 271, Transmittal No. 7467, released on April 6, 1979.
21. U.S. Postal Service v. Federal Communications Commission, D.C. Cir. No. 79-2243 (docketed October 18, 1979).
22. U.S., Postal Rate Commission, *Opinion and Recommended Decision*, Docket No. MC78-3 (Washington: Postal Rate Commission, December 17, 1979), pp. 6–15; 141.
23. *Ibid.*, pp. 6; 145–159.
24. U.S., Postal Service, Board of Governors, notice rejecting the recommended decision of the Postal Rate Commission in Docket No. MC78-3, typewritten, February 22, 1980, pp. 1–4.
25. U.S., Postal Rate Commission, *Opinion and Recommended Decision Upon Reconsideration*, Docket No. MC78-3 (Washington: Postal Rate Commission, April 8, 1980), pp. 3–19.

26. This argument comes from "Government Regulation of Government: The USPS, the PRC and the FCC," *Regulation* (May/June 1980), p. 8.

27. *Washington Post*, August 16, 1980, p. F7.

28. "Government Regulation of Government," p. 9.

29. See James Q. Wilson and Patricia Rachal, "Can the Government Regulate Itself?" *Public Interest*, no. 46 (Winter 1977), p. 4.

30. U.S., Postal Service, *Annual Report of the Postmaster General, Fiscal 1979*, p. 27; U.S., Postal Service, "Comprehensive Statement on Postal Operations" (January 1980), Appendix, p. 5.

31. See Daniel Greenberg, "Without the Stamp of Research," *Washington Post*, February 12, 1980, p. A19.

32. Peter F. Drucker, *Management: Tasks, Responsibilities, Practices* (New York: Harper & Row, 1974), chap. 7, esp. p. 77.

Chapter 9

MANAGING THE POSTAL SERVICE: PROBLEMS AND PROSPECTS

The 1970 postal reorganization transformed the legal and institutional arrangements of postal policymaking machinery. These changes were the most extensive in the postal system's history and among the most extensive ever for any federal executive agency. The reorganization was a highly conspicuous effort by the federal government to improve the management and performance of the nation's oldest and largest public enterprise. Despite the far-reaching changes, however, the Postal Service today continues to be the object of harsh official and public criticism.

To a great extent, these criticisms are unfair. Though the postal reorganization has certainly not achieved all its architects envisioned, it has in many ways been remarkably successful, allowing the Postal Service to make assorted improvements in services and managerial practices. For example, several internal reorganizations have decentralized decision-making authority and produced a more streamlined and effective management structure. Postal executives also have pushed hard to modernize and mechanize the physical plant of the Postal Service. As a result, by 1979 about 65 per cent of the mail processed in mechanized offices was being sorted mechanically, compared with 25 per cent before the reorganization. Moreover, the Area Mail Processing program has increased the volume of mail processed at central post offices, thereby enhancing the cost-effectiveness of the new high-speed equipment used in processing mail. Partly because of these efforts, the Postal Service has managed to reduce its workforce by about 65,000 from pre-reorganization levels, even though the annual volume of mail has increased by 13 billion pieces since 1971.[1]

At the same time, the Postal Service has successfully introduced two popular new services, Mailgram and Express Mail, and is laying the groundwork for the various electronic transmission services it will establish in the 1980s.

And although the soaring costs of operating the mail system have driven postal rates up sharply in recent years, the Postal Service has nevertheless kept postage rates significantly below those of other industrialized nations (except Canada, where postal services are heavily subsidized). Other countries' first-class postage rates (converted to U.S. dollars) in 1979 made our 15-cent rate seem inexpensive by comparison: Canada, 14.6 cents; Italy,. 20.9 cents; Japan, 21.1 cents; Great Britain, 22.0 cents; Switzerland, 25.1 cents; Belgium, 28.3 cents; Sweden, 31.1 cents; France, 32.0 cents; and West Germany, 34.6 cents.[2]

In short, there is plenty of evidence to counter the popular perception of the Postal Service as an unresponsive, profligate, ill-managed enterprise. But the perception remains. Politicians castigate postal executives for failing to control costs. Mail users complain about slow and inconsistent delivery, damaged parcels, high postage rates, and the like. It is hard to persuade stubborn and cynical observers that the continuing problems of the mail system (some of which are admittedly quite serious) cannot simply be attributed to poor management. Though the charge of organizational incompetence may be intuitively appealing, there are several other explanations that are more instructive and that strike closer to the truth. Some problems, for example, are simply inherent in the nature of the organization's monumental task of collecting, sorting, and delivering 100 billion pieces of mail a year. Others stem from economic and demographic forces that are beyond the control of postal executives. Still others are the consequence of performing this service in a governmental (which is to say, political) setting, where Congress has yet to make difficult but necessary choices among the Postal Service's currently conflicting goals.

Unrealistic Expectations

One reason the Postal Service has had great difficulty meeting the expectations held for it is that those expectations were unrealistic in the first place, inflated by the rhetoric of enthusiastic reformers who needed to convince others of the reorganization's virtues. To persuade Congress and the public that the 1970 reorganization was not only wise but necessary, postal reformers promised more than the new organizational setup could be certain to deliver. The reorganization's proponents unabashedly claimed that the new organization would cut costs, improve services, and remove the deficit. The reformers reinforced these optimistic expectations through a vigorous, highly organized campaign to sell the reorganization idea to elected officials and special-interest groups. And once Congress and the President adopted the plan, it was politically incumbent on them also to convince a still skeptical public that this was a great step toward better service at steadier rates. In short, there was a rhetorical spiral at work in the period before and immediately following the reorganization, pushing expectations well beyond what was likely under even the best conditions. But the conditions were not even good, much less the best. The postal system was in poor shape at the time of the reorganization, and the general economic conditions during the new Postal Service's first decade of life were hardly favorable to controlling costs or to a quick return to financial health.

A Legacy of Inefficiency

Some of the optimism about the likely effects of the postal reorganization stemmed from faulty extrapolations by postal reformers who expected that the benefits of the corporate form of organization were easily transferable to a 200-year-old bureaucracy.

In 1968, when staff members of the President's Commission on Postal Organization reviewed the structure, operation, and management of existing government corporations (for example, the TVA and the St. Lawrence Seaway Development Corporation), they discovered that all these enterprises were financially self-sustaining and effective in controlling their costs. So also were most of the government enterprises at the state level, such as state liquor stores and bridge and tunnel authorities. The clear assumption was that with the proper organizational design, the postal system also could be restored to fiscal health. But in truth the obstacles were staggering.

Not the least obstacle was that Postal Service executives were charged with righting a huge organization that had already been operating for nearly two centuries. The managers of the reconstituted Postal Service inherited an organizational legacy that included outmoded physical plants, an inflated workforce, rigid standard operating procedures, and a set of established expectations (both inside and outside the organization) about what the Postal Service should do and how it should be done. Most other government corporations and quasi-corporations have been established free of the burden of an organizational history. In virtually every other case of public enterprise at the federal level (except for Amtrak), these enterprises started with a clean slate, unburdened by past practices and expectations. But executives in the new Postal Service faced the task of trying to overcome the untoward effects of practices and services that had been established over many years to meet political needs rather than economic demands. Postal management thus inherited an organization with operating problems and deficit-producing services and obligations not of their making.

High Inflation

Another important factor complicating the Postal Service's fiscal recovery has been the unexpectedly high inflation rate in the 1970s, which has particularly affected this labor-intensive industry. For each of the last three labor contracts with the unions, for example, the obligations the Postal Service incurred under the cost-of-living adjustment provision have amounted to more than the negotiated "up-front" wage increases. Moreover, inflation has been a big factor in pushing the Postal Service's costs for its employee's coverage under the Civil Service Retirement program from $445 million in fiscal 1972 to $1.4 billion in 1979.[3]

The soaring cost of fuel has also placed severe pressure on the postal budget, increasing the cost of heating the system's 30,500 post offices and dramatically hiking the costs of operating its fleet of

203,000 vehicles; each penny-a-gallon increase in gasoline prices costs the Postal Service $3.5 million annually.[4]

Another cost factor largely beyond the effective control of postal executives is the annual increase in the number of delivery addresses. That number increases by more than 2 per cent each year as the population expands, as new businesses are established, and as new families set up their homes. The number of delivery addresses has increased from 67.3 million in 1971 to approximately 82 million in 1979. The Postal Service has no choice but to serve these new addresses, thus consuming more fuel and manpower.[5]

In short, some of the financial problems of the Postal Service stem from the legacy of inefficient and costly operations it inherited, while others are tied to the high rate of inflation in the 1970s and the costs of serving an ever-expanding delivery network.

Some Prescriptions and Prognoses

Though solutions to most of these problems are largely outside the direct reach of postal management, there are nevertheless a number of important steps that could be taken to place the postal system on a firmer footing. First, the Postal Service should significantly increase its expenditures for research and technological development. Industrial retardation has long been the Achilles' heel of the postal system and will continue to be so as long as postal management devotes only one-tenth of 1 per cent of the postal budget to developing new technology. The crippling labor-intensity of postal operations requires that the Postal Service move ahead aggressively in its search for labor-saving technological breakthroughs.[6]

The Postal Service should make greater use of optical character reading equipment and bar codes to improve the efficiency of mail-processing and to control costs. Similarly, postal executives should not be swayed from their plans for a nine-digit Zip Code by carping members of Congress or writers of newspaper editorials. The expanded Zip Code, when fully implemented, will help control Postal Service expenses and will permit more efficient processing of mail.

Second, the Postal Service and the Postal Rate Commission should cease the cross-subsidization practices that are an inherent part of current methods of accounting for costs and setting rates. To improve its cost identification (and thereby improve pricing), the Postal Service should adopt functional cost analysis; that is, it should examine costs in terms of principal cost components such as carrier street time, speed of delivery, distance, size, and weight.[7] We have seen that the Postal Service recently has been slowly improving its cost attributions, but more needs to be done in this area. First-class mailers should not be forced to shoulder costs incurred by other classes of mail. Not only is this unfair and contrary to the intent of the 1970 reorganization, but it encourages inefficient use of resources.[8]

The Postal Rate Commission so far has been indulgent of Postal Service costing and pricing methods. Perhaps the PRC would be more independent and vigorous in performing its tasks if the anomalous arrangements under which the agency is now funded were changed. Under one of the most curious setups yet devised for funding a regulatory agency, the PRC now receives its operating finances from the Postal Service Fund, based on a budget submitted to the Governors of the Postal Service. This practice is unsound and needs to be changed. The expenses of the PRC should be paid, just as for most other federal regulatory agencies, with appropriations from Congress, set through the normal budgetary process.[9]

Third, steps must be taken to bring spiraling postal wages under control. Postal policymakers should end the current practice of using the same wage structure across the entire country. This uniform wage schedule provides postal workers in small towns and rural areas with wages that are often far greater than those received by privately employed workers with similar skills and, in some cases, even greater than highly trained professionals in those areas. This practice also inequitably compensates postal workers in some of the large cities where the cost of living is high and the job pressures great. The Postal Service should use labor market data provided by the Bureau of Labor Statistics to revise the postal wage structure in a way that accounts for differentials in local labor market wages. This change would produce substantial economies and greater equity.[10]

In addition, postal executives must dedicate themselves in coming contract negotiations to a much harder line than they have previously adopted. Most important of all in the short run, the Postal Service must at least find a way to put a limit on the cost-of-living adjustments paid to postal workers beyond their regular wage increases. If the Postal Service proves unsuccessful in holding the line in contract negotiations, Congress should end the postal system's collective bargaining experiment and place responsibility for setting postal wages with an independent pay board or, preferably, with the Postal Rate Commission—a solution that would have the advantage of maintaining some linkage between revenues and expenditures.

But even if all these measures are adopted, a lasting "solution" to the postal problem will be found only if members of Congress make explicit their preference on a basic policy question that is still unanswered in practice ten years after the reorganization: whether our goal is to maintain the postal system as a public service with many special constituencies being subsidized, or to operate it as an efficient delivery system that keeps costs in check and charges rates based on costs. This is by no means an easy choice, as evidenced by the long-standing unwillingness of Congress to face up to it. Each alternative entails great costs of one sort or another—social, economic, or political.

If members of Congress determine that the present array of traditional postal services is essential to national needs (or to their own electoral fortunes), the Postal Service can certainly provide these services. But the financial costs will continue to soar, and as they do the large businesses that generate most of the mail (and thus most postal revenues) will search for less costly alternatives to the Postal Service. The loss of this business will generate still higher unit costs and higher rates, thus accelerating the cycle of cumulative deterioration in the postal system. Congress may, of course, choose to subsidize the traditional postal services. But the long-term economic costs of a full subsidy policy would be staggering; maintaining the current system would cost tens of billions of dollars over the next decade. Moreover, increased subsidies would encourage slack management and reduce the incentive for the Postal Service to try to balance its costs and revenues.

If, on the other hand, members of Congress should decide seriously that they want a cost-effective mail system that will be lean and responsive to fast-changing developments in its environment, they must give postal executives the free hand they need to produce that kind of system. The attendant political costs would, of course, be great, since postal executives would likely begin by instituting higher rates for some services or by pruning the system of traditional services and practices currently maintained only to meet political needs, not economic demands. Postal officials know, for example, that they could trim the system's costs by at least $2.3 billion annually by (1) replacing door delivery whenever possible with curbline or cluster-box delivery (a saving of $210 million); (2) reducing the frequency of delivery from six days to five days for businesses and three days for residences (a saving of $1.15 billion); (3) changing service standards to permit more mail to be processed during day shifts (a saving of $392 million); and (4) replacing uneconomical post offices with less expensive forms of service (a saving of $567 million).[11]

Political Constraints

Despite the stated intent of the 1970 Postal Reorganization Act, members of Congress to date have chosen to place limits on postal executives' freedom to pursue efficiency and economy, especially when the savings might come at the price of lessened public convenience. For example, as we saw in Chapter 3, when the Postal Service has tried to cut costs by adopting cluster-box delivery in some suburban areas or by replacing small, uneconomical post offices with less expensive forms of service, postal executives have found their efforts blocked by groups (often the Postal Service's own employees) whose influence on Capitol Hill is strong enough to win congressional intervention.

The Postal Service's experiences since 1971 indicate that trying to "take politics out of the Post Office"—the rallying cry of the reorganization's advocates—was in many ways an exercise in futility. The postal system is imbued with a decidedly political character that even the most determined reformers could not exorcise. The nature of postal services and operations (especially the immediacy and visibility of mail services to citizens), along with the organizational strength of the special interests attentive to postal policy, together guarantee that the mail system will continue to attract close scrutiny by elected officials.

Although the reorganization act made some important alterations in the institutions and procedures governing postal policymaking, it did not substantially alter the interests, goals, or demands of the organizations and groups that compose the postal policy arena. The unions continue to view themselves as entitled to all the benefits other federal employees have even though the unions possess privileges these others do not share. The mailing industries continue to argue that their operations merit subsidized rates. And citizens continue to see mail delivery services as a political birthright—a service whose features are not to be tampered with. All this highlights a management and policy problem common to many governmental services, not just mail delivery. Once a benefit or service is provided by the government, taking it away is very difficult. The benefits or services provided by a government agency create over time a set of dependencies, and even more, a set of expectations and demands. If a pattern of service (such as six-day mail delivery) has existed for a long time, everyone comes to assume that it is inviolable—the natural and correct way of doing things.[12] These fixed expectations are what postal executives confront in trying to fashion a leaner, more cost-effective, and more economically rational postal system. Congress requires the Postal Service to continue supplying certain services, not because of economic demands but because of established expectations, backed up by political demands.

Congress continues to accede to these pressures because the same political incentives that led legislators to agree to the reorganization in the first place persist today. In the postal policy arena, members of Congress find it easiest simply to give people what they want; there is no political incentive for members of Congress to face up to hard policy decisions. The nature of postal services is such that the benefits of service cutbacks would be widely dispersed among the people at large and, thus, barely noticed by them. The costs, however, would be either highly concentrated (as in communities where post offices are closed) or widely dispersed but still keenly felt (as with less frequent deliveries).[13] Since there is, in any case, no electoral gain (and there are potentially large electoral losses) involved in going along with the Postal Service efforts to economize, most members of Congress act instead to accommodate the demands of special interests and to satisfy the established expectations of the mail-receiving public.

In the process, Congress leaves the Postal Service trying to serve a wide variety of economically irreconcilable social and political objectives: frequent, speedy and consistent delivery; universally available letter-mail services at reasonable and uniform rates; support of a large and well-paid workforce; continuation of an expensive rural network; maintenance of numerous collection and distribution points; and also the mandate to accomplish all this without a deficit. Clearly not all of these goals can be achieved, but the Postal Service, as a governmental organization, has no choice but to attend to them anyway. This complicates the conduct of "businesslike" management, since there is no way, because of the political pressures and the absence of a market for reconciling impersonally conflicting wants, that these competing goals can be reconciled or reasonable trade-offs among them negotiated.

Under these circumstances, the Postal Service is bound to be a continuing source of frustration and dissatisfaction to its assorted constituencies, all of whom are demanding too many conflicting results from it. Postal management cannot solve this problem by itself, nor are there any administrative panaceas that will lead to a solution. Just as with the bureaucracy problem in general, "the only point at which very much leverage can be gained on the problem is when we decide what it is we are trying to accomplish." [14] Congress alone can solve this problem, and it can do so only by making difficult choices among currently irreconcilable goals. Members of Congress will have to move beyond their stock harangues at postal management and decide whether they want a costly postal service that meets an assortment of conspicuous political needs or whether they want a lean and cost-effective mail delivery system that will fit more cleanly in a changing communications environment.

Endnotes

1. U.S. Postal Service, *History of the U.S. Postal Service, 1775–1979*, Postal Service Publication 100, May 1980, p. 11.
2. U.S. Postal Service, *Comprehensive Statement on Postal Operations*, January 1980, p. 15.
3. U.S. Postal Service, *Annual Report of the Postmaster General, 1971–1972*, p. 32; U.S. Postal Service, *Annual Report of the Postmaster General, Fiscal 1979*, p. 21.
4. Larry Light, "Will Congress Seek More Control of the Mail Service?" *Congressional Quarterly Weekly Report*, March 3, 1979, p. 378.
5. Commission on Postal Service, *Report of the Commission on Postal Service* (Washington: U.S. Government Printing Office, 1977), vol. 1, p. 15.

6. This recommendation, like some of those that follow, is one of the dominant prescriptions appearing in most contemporary analyses of the postal system's problems. See *ibid.*, pp. 80, 81.

7. See James C. Miller and Roger Sherman, "Has the Act Been Fair to Mailers?" in Roger Sherman, ed., *Perspectives on Postal Service Issues* (Washington: American Enterprise Institute, 1980), p. 67.

8. See Alan L. Sorkin, *The Economics of the Postal System* (Lexington, Mass.: Lexington Books, 1980), p. 182.

9. See Commission on Postal Service, *Report of the Commission on Postal Service*, vol. 1, pp. 78–79.

10. Sorkin, *Economics of the Postal System*, pp. 183–184.

11. Commission on Postal Service, *Report of the Commission on Postal Service*, vol. 2, pp. 758–759.

12. See Robert D. Behn and Kim Sperduto, "Medical Schools and the 'Entitlement Ethic,' " *Public Interest*, no. 57 (Fall 1979), p. 55.

13. James Q. Wilson has argued that we can understand how society deals with different public policy areas by examining how costs and benefits of the policy area in question are distributed. See James Q. Wilson, *Political Organizations* (New York: Basic Books, 1973), pp. 331–337.

14. James Q. Wilson, "The Bureaucracy Problem," in Alan A. Altshuler, ed., *The Politics of the Federal Bureaucracy* (New York: Dodd, Mead and Co., 1968), p. 30.

INDEX